An English Reader's Guide to the French Legal System

This wholly original interdisciplinary study combines a theoretical approach to legal translation with a practical exposition of how the relevant principles may be applied to the French legal system, to which it provides a thorough introduction.

In three preliminary chapters the author discusses what is meant by 'legal language', expounds the techniques available for translating legal (or any other culture-specific) terms and considers practical aspects of legal translation. The remaining five chapters describe the French legal system in detail – the branches of the law, legislation, the courts, the legal professions and criminal procedure and penalties – and include all the relevant French legal terms together with suggested English renderings.

The book thus simultaneously provides an up-to-date account of the French legal system and a methodical, discursive treatment of the problems of translating the associated terminology into English. Diagrams and an index of over 450 key terms make it an invaluable reference work not only for trainee and practising translators but also for students of French law, legal practitioners, diplomats, journalists and anyone else with a professional or academic interest in France's legal institutions. Its publication is especially timely as the European Community moves towards the creation of a single market by the end of 1992 and British businessmen and lawyers find themselves increasingly involved with Continental legal systems.

Martin Weston has many years' experience of translation in the Secretariat of the Council of Europe in Strasbourg and is currently Senior Translator in the Registry of the European Court of Human Rights.

An English Reader's Guide to the French Legal System

Martin Weston

BERG
New York / Oxford
Distributed exclusively in the US and Canada by
St Martin's Press, New York

First Published in 1991 by
Berg Publishers Limited
Editorial Offices
165 Taber Avenue, Providence, R.I. 02906, USA
150 Cowley Road, Oxford OX4 1JJ, UK

Library of Congress Cataloging-in-Publication Data

Weston, Martin.
An English reader's guide to the French legal system / Martin Weston.
p. cm.
Includes bibliographical references and index.
ISBN 0–85496–642–0
1. Law—France. I. Title.
KJV234.W47 1990
349.44—dc20
[344.4] 90–37067
CIP

British Library Cataloguing in Publication Data

Weston, Martin
An English reader's guide to the French legal system.
1. France. Law
I. Title
344.4

ISBN 0–85496–642–0

Printed and bound in Great Britain by Billing and Sons Ltd, Worcester

For my mother

Contents

Diagrams

Preface

The original draft of this book was submitted in 1983 as a dissertation towards the degree of Master of Arts in General and Applied Linguistics at the University of Exeter, and I should like to thank the University both for the very enjoyable year spent there in 1980/81 and for its generous award of a postgraduate scholarship. I am also most grateful for the year's leave of absence from the Council of Europe Secretariat, without which it would not have been possible to read for the degree.

For information and advice on (mainly) legal aspects of this study, as well as for their encouragement, I am much indebted to my colleagues Hans-Jürgen Bartsch, Vincent Berger and Frank Bridge (the last-mentioned recently retired), and to Bernard Rudden, Professor of Comparative Law in the University of Oxford. All of them also kindly read and commented on the final draft of the original dissertation. For any remaining errors – as well as any added during the process of substantial revision and expansion for publication – and for the views expressed in the text as it now stands I am, of course, alone responsible. Without Frank Bridge's assistance with legal translation over many years and, in particular, the use of the splendid French–English legal dictionary he has compiled, I could never have specialised in this field. Thanks are due also to Andrew Drzemczewski and other colleagues and friends, too numerous to mention by name, who have helped and encouraged in various ways, especially by drawing my attention to relevant newspaper and periodical articles, nearly all of which I have made use of.

Last but not least, I should like to express my gratitude to the University of Oxford, without whose education and continuing hospitality I would never have been in a position to write even so modest a book.

Martin Weston
Strasbourg, January 1990

Introduction

This book sets out to propose general guidelines for the translation of legal texts and to offer English translations of key terms in selected areas of one of the civil-law – or Romano-Germanic – systems, which it describes in some detail. The French legal system has the advantage of being in a sense paradigmatic, for, as is pointed out in Amos and Walton's *An Introduction to French Law*, 'there can be no doubt that a study of French law provides the most convenient line of approach to these various laws. [. . .] To become familiar with the law of France is to learn a *lingua franca*, and to be initiated into ideas which are common to a great part of the non-Anglo-Saxon legal world'.[1]

Accordingly, the *Guide* is primarily a manual of translation practice rather than an exercise in translation theory like Georges Mounin's *Les Problèmes théoriques de la traduction* or J. C. Catford's *A Linguistic Theory of Translation*, being theoretical only in so far as it is concerned with approaching the translation of culture-specific concepts *systematically*. It is noteworthy that Mounin made clear in a later article that modern linguistics has really very little more to contribute than has traditional philology to the study or translation of legal language, other than an example of scientific method and a number of relevant concepts, such as 'sign', 'structure' and 'system'.[2]

Newmark has gone so far as to claim that 'purely theoretical treatises on translation are even less profitable than most purely theoretical treatises. In spite of the claims of Nida and the Leipzig translation school, who start writing on translation where others leave off, there is no such thing as a science of translation and never will be.'[3] The validity of this apparently extreme view, however,

1. Sir Maurice Amos and F. P. Walton, *An Introduction to French Law*, 3rd edn by F. H. Lawson, A. E. Anton and L. N. Brown (Oxford University Press, 1967), pp. 2 and 5.

2. Georges Mounin, 'La linguistique comme science auxiliaire dans les disciplines juridiques', *Meta*, 24 (1979), 9–17.

3. P. P. Newmark, 'Twenty-three restricted rules of translation', *Incorporated Linguist*, 12 (1973), 9–15 (p. 9).

depends on what Newmark means by 'purely theoretical', and the statement hardly does justice to his own theoretical work.

A more specific criticism of much modern translation theory (and undeniably a just one) is made by Werner Koller in his introduction to translation theory: 'It cannot be denied that one or two contributions to translation theory display such a marked degree of abstraction, at any rate in their terminology, that the translator finds himself wondering what it can all possibly have to do with his work and with his problems and experiences.'[4] More damningly still, Helmut Winter has summed up: 'After a period of euphoria, when it was thought that the concept of equivalence had been accurately defined and the key to the central problem of translation thus found, the level of these contributions [to translation theory] dropped back to one of hollow-sounding platitudes and jargon-ridden restatements of the obvious.'[5] And he refers to 'the inability of a would-be science to provide those whose business is translation with even remotely useful insights'.[6]

In its determinedly practical orientation – if perhaps in no other way – the *Guide* has, I hope, something in common with Jean Delisle's splendid book *L'Analyse du discours comme méthode de traduction*, than which it is much more specialised, however: I have here studied only one rather technical corner of the category of translation that Delisle terms '*textes pragmatiques*' – and I would in fact argue that legal translation is a separate category in its own right.[7]

While occasional articles have appeared – notably by Newmark – suggesting various practical approaches to the translation of sundry culture-specific terms, such studies have been tentative and only

4. 'Es kann nicht in Abrede gestellt werden, daß einzelne Beiträge zur Übersetzungswissenschaft sich durch eine solche Abstraktheit, mindestens in der Terminologie, auszeichnen, daß sich der Übersetzer fragt, was das noch mit seiner Tätigkeit und seinen Problemen und Erfahrungen zu tun haben könnte.' W. Koller, *Einführung in die Übersetzungswissenschaft*, 3rd edn (Quelle & Meyer, 1987), pp. 44–5.

5. 'Diese Bemühungen [um die Theorie des Übersetzens] sind nach einer Phase der Euphorie, in der man den Begriff der Äquivalenz präzise definiert und damit den Schlüssel zum Kernproblem des Übersetzens gefunden [zu] haben glaubte, wieder auf die Stufe hohltönender Platitüden, jargonbefrachteter Umschreibungen des Selbstverständlichen zurückgefallen.' H. Winter, 'Die Schokoladentorte zwickt an mir', *Frankfurter Allgemeine Zeitung*, 16 October 1981, p. 25.

6. '[. . .] die Unfähigkeit einer Möchtegernwissenschaft, denjenigen, die mit dem Geschäft des Übersetzens zu tun haben, auch nur halbwegs brauchbare Einsichten an die Hand zu geben.' Ibid.

7. The evidence to support this view is briefly set out in my article 'The role of translation at the European Court of Human Rights', in F. Matscher and H. Petzold, eds, *Protecting Human Rights: The European Dimension. Studies in honour of Gérard J. Wiarda . . .* (Carl Heymanns Verlag, 1988), pp. 679–89 (pp. 681–2).

perfunctorily illustrated by more or less arbitrarily chosen examples from a variety of otherwise unrelated fields. They are quite inadequate to meet the needs of translators (particularly those who are not lawyers or who are inexperienced) faced with any kind of legal text. At the same time, the few books on the French legal system written in English by comparative lawyers have naturally focused on explaining the system itself and have paid scant attention to the translation of the terms and institutions they discuss; and as, moreover, their authors have not (one must assume) been trained linguists or professional translators, the result has in some cases been that their chosen English terminology is either meaningless to a native English reader or at best unnecessarily opaque, quaint or misleading.

There consequently remains a conspicuous need for a methodical consideration of the difficulties of 'pragmatic' translation field by field. Koller is rightly of the opinion that

> translating as many texts as possible more or less mechanically, discussing random examples of language use or subject-matter and unsystematically stringing translation difficulties together cannot suffice to build up translation competence rationally and effectively. What needs to be done is rather to set out and teach translation examples systematically [. . .]. It is also sensible for translation examples to be systematically analysed within whole categories of text (such as political texts, medical texts, advertising texts, poetical texts).[8]

The present work – based on stated principles – is intended as the first contribution to a systematic treatment of the legal field. Although obviously it is impossible to cover the whole area of the law in a book of modest proportions and I have perforce had to be selective, I have aimed to include the main aspects in a logical order and discuss the key terms of each in turn, rather than just pick out terms at random for the purposes of illustration. I have described the French legal system as it stands, to the best of my knowledge, at the beginning of 1990.

While the study is by definition comparative and unashamedly

8. 'Ein sinnvoller und effektiver Aufbau der übersetzerischen Kompetenz kann [. . .] nur unzulänglich durch das mehr oder weniger mechanische Übersetzen möglichst vieler Texte, die unzusammenhängende Behandlung von sprachlichen und sachlichen Einzelfällen, die unsystematische Aneinanderreihung von Übersetzungsschwierigkeiten erfolgen. Es geht vielmehr darum, Übersetzungsfälle und -schwierigkeiten systematisch aufzuarbeiten und zu vermitteln; [. . .]. Sinnvoll ist es auch, wenn die Übersetzungsfälle systematisch innerhalb ganzer Textgattungen (etwa politische Texte, Texte der Medizin, Werbetexte, poetische Texte) analysiert werden.' Koller, *Einführung*, p. 45.

interdisciplinary rather than purely linguistic, it does not, of course, aspire to be a treatise on comparative law; but since no up-to-date account of the French legal system is currently available in English, my hope is that it may none the less serve as an elementary introduction for students embarking on a study of the French legal system and help them to get a proper grasp of some of the basic concepts – for there is a need on the lawyers' side here too, as was recognised half a century ago by the late H. C. Gutteridge, formerly Professor of Comparative Law in the University of Cambridge, when he wrote: 'I would, in fact, be disposed to assert that pitfalls of terminology are the greatest difficulty and danger which the student of comparative law encounters in his novitiate.'[9] So far as I am aware, no book on law any more than on translation has ever tackled this primarily linguistic task: English works on French and comparative law are curiously silent about the translation problem or at most mention it in passing. Yet surely it is plain that English-speaking students of the law of a foreign country are unlikely to gain a true understanding of the foreign concepts unless given accurate translations, and that translators cannot provide accurate translations unless they have a clear idea of the overall system into which particular concepts fit; the generally poor translations offered by non-linguist lawyers and non-lawyer linguists afford ample evidence of this.

It is perhaps not inappropriate that this attempt to fulfil the need should at last have been made following the bicentenary year of the revolution that ushered in the essentials of France's legal system as it is today – a year, it must be added, that ended fittingly with its own historic revolutions in Eastern Europe. But in writing the book I have been looking not so much back to 1789 as forwards to 1993 and beyond, when, as was pointed out again not so long ago, there will be greater demand for legal services with an international dimension 'in the new and very challenging atmosphere where EC law will be increasingly central and conflicts with local national regulations or interpretations thereof will abound'.[10] More generally, the *Guide* will also, I hope, prove useful to diplomats and other civil servants dealing with French and Community affairs, as well as to students of French institutions.

Readers who are not themselves engaged in translation may prefer to skip Chapter 1, which is written more particularly for

9. H. C. Gutteridge, 'The comparative aspects of legal terminology', *Tulane Law Review*, 12 (1938), 401–11 (p. 403).

10. Nigel Reeves, '1992 Languages: the barrier no EC directive can eliminate', *Linguist*, 28 (1989), 2–7 (p. 5).

linguists – though I have deliberately avoided being too technical in it. But they would be well advised to read Chapter 2 if they wish to have a full understanding of the approach adopted to the translation of terms in Part II. Some rudimentary understanding of the English legal system is taken for granted in Part II – though probably not more than could be acquired from reading the relevant chapters of an introduction to English law such as the one listed in the bibliography at the end of the book – but no previous knowledge of the French system is assumed. For all readers a full index is given of all the French terms discussed, so that their English translations can rapidly be found, together with the description of the institutions, persons or procedures they denote; the *Guide* may thus also be used as a reference book.

It may be asked – especially, perhaps, by lawyers – whether the needs alluded to above have not already been substantially met by the (few) bilingual or multilingual legal dictionaries on the market. As will be pointed out in due course, however, those available hitherto have not by any means been as helpful as might be thought by anyone who has not had occasion to consult them at all regularly.

Note on typographical conventions

Throughout the text (but not in the all-French index) French words and expressions other than in quotations or the titles of articles are italicised (and printed in accordance with French conventions of capitalisation, etc.) whether they are being used or – more commonly – merely discussed, while English words and expressions are placed between single inverted commas when they are being discussed (e.g. as translations of French terms). Single inverted commas are also used for all quotations (as is normal practice) and occasionally when English technical terms are introduced; but no confusion is likely to arise. Where French terms are adopted in English for want of any adequate native English translation (see sections 2.1 and 2.4), however, they are *not* italicised (though they no doubt would be in an actual English translation of a French text) and they are consequently then printed to accord with English conventions of capitalisation, etc.; this is in order to maximise clarity by distinguishing, for the purposes of exposition, between 'original' French words as instances of source language requiring translation and French words adopted (transcribed) in an English translation.

PART I

Theoretical and practical approaches to translation

–1–

The linguistic issues

1.1 Conceptual differences between languages

The fundamental difficulty in translation of any kind is how to overcome conceptual difference. The challenge has been succinctly formulated by Koller: 'Human languages embody in their signs different conceptual systems reflecting their individual histories, and the problem of translation is that despite these differences the attempt has to be made to transfer what has been (or could be) thought in the other language to one's own language.'[1] This general problem becomes particularly acute when the translator has to render into the target or translation language (hereafter referred to as the TL) concepts which differ from those familiar to its speakers not merely in minor denotational (referential, cognitive) attributes or in connotation but primarily for cultural and – more specifically – institutional reasons. Stated baldly: ' A word denoting an object, an institution or, if such exists, a psychological characteristic peculiar to the source-language culture is always more or less untranslatable – everything else is more or less translatable.'[2]

Thus translating *maison*[3] as either 'house' or 'home' does not usually entail undue difficulties of choice, because although *maison* is not congruent in denotation or connotation with either of the English words, both French speakers and English speakers do recognisably have *maisons*/houses/homes, of whatever kind, and the differences between the terms are subordinate to that basic fact, the choice between these two particular TL possibilities being a

1. 'Die menschlichen Sprachen erfassen in ihren Zeichen je einzelsprachlich und historisch unterschiedliche Begriffssysteme; das Problem des Übersetzens besteht darin, daß trotz dieser Unterschiedlichkeit versucht werden muß, das in der anderen Gedachte (und Denkbare) in die eigene Sprache zu überführen.' W. Koller, *Einführung in die Übersetzungswissenschaft*, 3rd edn (Quelle & Meyer, 1987), p. 69.

2. P. P. Newmark, 'Twenty-three restricted rules of translation', *Incorporated Linguist*, 12 (1973), 9–15 (p. 12).

3. Although this book is nominally concerned only with legal translation, I have not hesitated, in Chapters 1 and 2, to draw my examples from other fields too, by way of illustrating the wider validity of the points made.

matter of connotational emphasis as often as not (but not always: contrast, for example, *maison de retraite* with *maison de poupée*). Translating *croissant*, on the other hand, is just not possible, because English-speaking countries simply do not traditionally bake croissants; the institution (if a croissant can be so described!) does not have a counterpart in the TL culture, and so the term for it must be transcribed and/or explained. (In the case of *croissant* the object has of course become sufficiently familiar for its lexical label to have been adopted in English as a borrowing no longer requiring a gloss, i.e. it has become naturalised.)

The two examples just adduced are, moreover, both concrete percepts; in the case of intellectual constructs, such as human institutions essentially are, the lack of congruence between languages is even greater. In some instances there will not even be an equivalent vocabulary in the TL, because the relevant sphere of activity (e.g. cricket, bullfighting) does not exist in the TL culture. Here again, translation is simply impossible, other than in metaphorical uses of the terminology concerned, when functionally equivalent metaphors can be found in the TL – a point perhaps worth stressing. For example, 'He was bowled out middle stump' might become 'On l'a réduit à quia', 'On l'a écrasé' or 'On l'a démoli'.

This problem confronts the translator whether the text to be translated is biblical, literary or 'general-purpose'.[4] Only in two specific kinds of translation does the problem not arise, other than incidentally: (a) in scientific and certain other technical translation (e.g. economic, mathematical and musical – within the same musical tradition; but not legal), merely because the concepts concerned are shared the world over;[5] and (b) in the translation of public notices, etc., relating to activities common to the two cultures in

4. I.e. a non-literary and non-technical text, usually translated only once and purely for information purposes, the content being all-important and the style of little importance. The bulk of the texts translated in non-specialist international organisations fall into this category, which, possibly for this reason, is commonly referred to as 'conference translation' – a term, however, that is both too narrow and yet could also include technical translation. A better label perhaps is the one adopted by R. W. Brislin, the editor of *Translation. Applications and Research* (Gardner Press, 1976): 'pragmatic translation'; and, as noted earlier, Jean Delisle likewise adopts the term '*textes pragmatiques*' in his *L'Analyse du discours comme méthode de traduction* (Éditions de l'Université d'Ottawa, 1980). Newmark talks of 'informative' texts. My own preference would be for describing this category as 'informational translation'.

5. Cf. G. Mounin: 'plus les traits sémantiquement pertinents d'une situation sont limitativement décrits, définis, et comptés (ce qui est le cas dans tous les domaines scientifiques), plus la traduction est possible et complète'. *Les Problèmes théoriques de la traduction* (Gallimard, 1963), p. 265.

question – where the contextually equivalent formula is mandatory (e.g. *défense de fumer* can only be translated as 'No smoking'). By contrast, the difficulty is perhaps encountered with particular frequency in administrative and similar texts, which often mention culture-specific institutions, official bodies and procedures.

The legal system is clearly a major institution and intellectual construct in any advanced society, and it gives rise to a characteristic 'culture-bound' style of language, normally described in linguistic terms as 'legal register'. Different legal registers and systems furnish an unusually good illustration of Sapir's somewhat dubious general contention in his 1929 essay 'The Status of Linguistics as a Science' that 'No two languages are ever sufficiently similar to be considered as representing the same social reality. The worlds in which different societies live are distinct worlds, not merely the same world with different labels attached.'[6] For, as Lucie Lauzière points out in an article entitled 'Un Vocabulaire juridique bilingue canadien', 'Il n'existe pas de vocabulaire scientifique commun à tous les systèmes juridiques du monde entier [. . .]. Contrairement aux sciences exactes qui se rapportent à des procédés ou à des principes absolus et reconnus universellement, le droit se fonde sur des relations très nuancées. Le vocabulaire juridique possède une valeur variable et relative au système juridique qui l'élabore.'[7] But what exactly is a 'register'? And is it accurate to speak of a 'legal register'?

1.2 Registers and their nature

The term 'register' appears to have been coined – somewhat surprisingly, perhaps – by the former Professor of the Romance Languages at Oxford University, T. B. W. Reid, in a 1956 article entitled 'Linguistics, structuralism and philology';[8] and eight years later Halliday, McIntosh and Strevens commented that work on English registers had only just begun.[9] Indeed, it can still be said today that, apart from Crystal and Davy's standard work *Investigating*

6. E. Sapir, *Selected Writings in Language, Culture and Personality*, D. G. Mandelbaum, ed. (University of California Press, 1949), p. 162.

7. L. Lauzière, 'Un Vocabulaire juridique bilingue canadien', *Meta*, 24 (1979), 109–14 (p. 111).

8. See J. Ellis and J. N. Ure, 'Registers', in *A Reader on Language Variety*, C. S. Butler and R. R. K. Hartmann, eds (University of Exeter, 1976, repr. 1979), pp. 32–40 (p. 32).

9. M. A. K. Halliday, A. McIntosh and P. D. Strevens, *The Linguistic Sciences and Language Teaching* (Longman, 1964), p. 40.

English Style and Geoffrey Leech's *English in Advertising*,[10] the practical study of register remains fragmentary and its theoretical study barely touched upon: the nature of the minimum unit of register – the utterance, perhaps, or the text? – does not seem even to have been considered, for example.

A language 'variety' has been neatly and simply defined by Halliday, McIntosh and Strevens as 'the language activity of one user in one use'.[11] In other words, a language variety will comprise 'dialectal' variation according to user – depending on (historical and geographical) community, social class, level of education, occupation, age and sex; and 'diatypic' variation according to use – depending on situation. It is the latter type of variation which is known as 'register'.

Register is linguistic *form*, not substance (phonic or graphic). As Halliday, McIntosh and Strevens put it in 1964 – obviously rightly, it seems to me: 'Dialects tend to differ primarily – and always to some extent – in substance. Registers, on the other hand, differ primarily in form.'[12] In other words, registers are defined and recognised chiefly by their formal properties, i.e. by their grammar and lexis – although a few (e.g. baby talk, liturgy) may be marked also by phonetic features such as intonation. Equally clearly, register is situated on the expression plane of language, not the content or meaning plane, i.e. is a way of talking about something and not the range of matters one chooses to talk about. As such, it must fall within the domain of stylistics and pragmatics rather than semantics. Halliday and Hasan's later statements on the subject in their *Cohesion in English* are therefore puzzling, notably: 'The register is the set of meanings, the configuration of semantic patterns, that are typically drawn upon under the specified conditions, along with the words and structures that are used in the realisation of these meanings.'[13]

The situational variables which largely determine language register may be most conveniently and simply labelled as 'field' (i.e. the subject of discussion or the nature of the activity which the language accompanies), 'mode' (broadly, written or spoken), 'function' (i.e. the purpose of the language produced) and (degree of) 'formality'. A given register will reflect a combination of points

10. D. Crystal and D. Davy, *Investigating English Style* (Longman, 1969); G. Leech, *English in Advertising: a Linguistic Study of Advertising in Great Britain* (Longman, 1966).
11. Halliday, McIntosh and Strevens, *The Linguistic Sciences*, p. 98.
12. Ibid., p. 88.
13. M. A. K. Halliday and R. Hasan, *Cohesion in English* (Longman, 1976), p. 23.

in these situational dimensions. (In more precise Hallidayan terms, 'field', 'mode', 'function' and 'formality' would be contextual categories linking groupings of linguistic features of immediate situation.)

Obviously 'field' (e.g. the law, medicine, sport) is a particularly important situational determinant of register and the more noticeable as it markedly influences the choice of lexical or 'content' words. This fact is doubtless responsible for the widespread but mistaken impression that register is exclusively a matter of vocabulary,[14] whereas vocabulary is merely the most conspicuous and readily identifiable feature of register. The true position is probably best summed up by Quirk et al.: 'Most typically, perhaps, the switch [from one register to another] involves nothing more than turning to the particular set of lexical items habitually used for handling the topic in question [. . .]. But there are grammatical correlates to subject-matter as well.'[15]

In so far as 'field' is the predominant situational factor determining register, it is of course true to say that selection of (cognitive) meanings does determine register to a large extent; but that is not at all the same thing as saying, with Halliday and Hasan, that register *is* the set of meanings. And 'mode', 'function' and 'formality' clearly are not selections of cognitive meanings, although one might acquiesce in Halliday's inclusion of the latter two in his category of 'interpersonal meaning'. Even in the case of 'field', Halliday, McIntosh and Strevens argued earlier that 'it is not the event or state of affairs being talked about that determines the choice [of language], but the convention that a certain kind of language is appropriate to a certain use'.[16]

In any case, Crystal and Davy have warned us that register is not determined wholly by identifiable features of the extra-linguistic situation: 'linguistic factors do not usually correlate in any neat one-for-one way with the situational variables in an extra-linguistic context. [. . .] [A]ny piece of discourse contains a large number of features which are difficult to relate to specific variables in the original extra-linguistic context, even though they may be felt to have some kind of stylistic value.'[17] After all, one has to bear in

14. A notable example of this view is provided by P. Trudgill on p. 101 of his *Sociolinguistics*, 2nd edn (Penguin, 1983): 'Registers are usually characterised solely by vocabulary differences.'

15. R. Quirk et al., *A Grammar of Contemporary English* (Longman, 1972, repr. 1979), p. 21.

16. Halliday, McIntosh and Strevens, *The Linguistic Sciences*, p. 87.

17. Crystal and Davy, *Investigating English Style*, p. 62.

mind that, as they pointed out, 'most of the segmental phonology of English [or any other language with a national standard] and most of the grammatical and lexical patterns are imposed on the language-user as being laws common to the whole community in all situations.'[18] And furthermore, in so far as register, like any other language variety, is subject to idiolectal variation, it can clearly vary among different participants in one and the same situation.

Similarly, Halliday, McIntosh and Strevens had already pointed out that – since registers are recognised by their formal properties – if two samples of language from what on non-linguistic grounds could be considered different situations showed no grammatical or lexical differences, then there could be no valid basis for assigning them to different registers: for the purposes of linguistic description, there would be only one situation type, not two.[19]

Conversely, much language that is commonly regarded as belonging to a single register (e.g. 'medical English') proves on inspection – indeed even *a priori* on reflection – to comprise several distinct registers. This, as will now be briefly demonstrated, applies to the so-called 'legal register'.

1.3 Legal register

The field of the law, as of other professions, embraces a wide range of activities and, accordingly, a wide range of language uses; so that the 'language of the law', just like, say, 'medical English (French, etc.)', is really a blanket term covering several distinct sub-varieties or sub-registers, each determined by differences in mode, function and formality within the same constant field (taking 'field' in its broadest sense as 'the law'; alternatively, it could be subdivided, e.g. into 'giving judgment', 'pleading in court', 'advising a client' and so on).

Thus in the legal field we may at the very least distinguish the major varieties of language used in the following situations:[20]

(1) professional discussions between solicitor or barrister and client (mode: spoken; functions: e.g. exposition, advice, sympathy; formality: neutral/formal);

18. Ibid., p. 65. See further p. 17 below.
19. Halliday, McIntosh and Strevens, *The Linguistic Sciences*, p. 89.
20. For ease of exposition I refer only to the English legal scene here, but with appropriate adjustment the analysis would be valid for any legal system.

(2) professional discussions between legal practitioners among themselves (mode: spoken; functions: various; formality: usually neutral or informal, maybe formal between junior and senior);

(3) judge giving judgment in court (mode: spoken or written-to-be-spoken;[21] functions: information, exposition, possibly literary; formality: formal);

(4) advocate pleading in court (mode: spoken; functions: persuasion, exposition, possibly flattery, provocation, etc.; formality: neutral/formal);

(5) legislation (mode: written; functions: regulation of conduct, injunction, archaism, etc.; formality: very formal).

Further distinctions could obviously be made, e.g. between a Crown Court judge addressing the jury or passing sentence; magistrates sitting in a juvenile court; the language of wills or of solicitors' letters threatening legal proceedings; and the language of legal treatises. But one should bear in mind that a line needs to be drawn somewhere and that, as Crystal and Davy point out in a memorable passage worth quoting at length,

> it is futile to continue sub-classifying situations when there are insufficient linguistic formal differences to warrant further analysis. 'Washing-powder advertising on television making use of a blue-eyed demonstrator on a Sunday' [. . .] would not be differentiated, one would hope, because it would not be very difficult to show that there was no significant language difference between this and the language used by other demonstrators of different ocular persuasions on other days of the week. Exactly how much sub-analysis can be justified is something yet to be decided: there is certainly no obvious cut-off point.[22]

21. Lyons would want to distinguish here between 'medium' (written or 'graphic') and 'channel' ('vocal-auditory'); see J. Lyons, *Semantics*, 2 vols (Cambridge University Press, 1977), pp. 69 and 581. Such a distinction between 'medium' and 'channel' – essentially the recognition that the spoken language can be written down and the written language spoken out loud – is obviously important, often useful, but not necessary for all purposes. The word 'medium', however, seems ill-chosen to make the distinction: I can make no sense of Lyons's statement (p. 581) that a judge addressing the jury '*will use the graphic medium*, as far as grammar and vocabulary are concerned, even though his utterance is transmitted along the vocal-auditory channel (and conforms to the phonological structure of the phonic medium)' (my italics). Surely he means 'graphic *style*' (using 'style' in its sense as a synonym for 'language variety')? I do not see how, even on a technical construction of the term 'medium', anything can sensibly be said to be in 'graphic medium' if it is not in fact written down.

22. Crystal and Davy, *Investigating English Style*, p. 72.

For the practical purposes of this study, however, it is quite clearly unnecessary to subdivide legal language into any sub-varieties at all: the theoretical point having been made that legal language is not a constant, uniform entity but comprises a number of 'styles' (in the narrow sense of 'register'), it is both legitimate and convenient for translation purposes to consider it as a whole as a single language register (contrasting, say, with medical language as a whole, which is equally subdivisible).

In any case, it is not the purpose of this study to examine and analyse the linguistic features of either English or French legal language. One general comment that certainly can be made, however, is that, in England at any rate, legal language has never fulfilled Bentham's requirement:

> It is further necessary that the laws should be as simple in style as in arrangement; that they should be expressed in the language ordinarily used; and that legal forms should be free from scientific jargon. If the style of the code be distinguishable from that of other books, it should be by its greater homeliness of diction; for it is designed to suit the comprehension of all men, and in particular of the class which is least enlightened.[23]

In relation specifically to the problem of translation, it is worth pointing out, as Mounin does in passing,[24] that technical registers in general (in this instance including the language of the law) are primarily denotative and not connotative.[25] This would apparently make legal translation easier, other things being equal; but, as has already been indicated, other things are not equal, because of the problem of culture specificity.

The basic problem in translating French legal texts into English is that France has a civil-law (Romano-Germanic) system, based in the first instance on the Napoleonic codes and ultimately derived

23. J. Bentham, *Theory of Legislation* (1802 in French; Oxford University Press, 1914), I, pp. 206–7, quoted in Sir Otto Kahn-Freund, C. Lévy and B. Rudden, *A Source-book on French Law*, 2nd edn (Clavendon Press, 1979), pp. 97–8.

24. '[. . .] l'opposition fondamentale entre langage ordinaire et terminologies techniques et scientifiques: l'existence, dans celui-là, l'inexistence dans celles-ci, de valeurs linguistiques spéciales, dites *connotations* [. . .]'; G. Mounin, *Les Problèmes théoriques de la traduction* (Gallimard, 1963), p. 143.

25. This means that for practical purposes it will be virtually unnecessary in the discussion of legal translation to make the distinction – often useful and even essential elsewhere – between, on the one hand, either full functional or purely formal equivalence of source-language and TL terms and, on the other, cognitive (i.e. denotative but not connotative) equivalence.

from Roman law, while England and Wales[26] have a common-law system. The result as regards translation is succinctly put by René David:

> To translate into English technical words used by lawyers in France, in Spain, or in Germany is in many cases an impossible task, and conversely there are no words in the languages of the continent to express the most elementary notions of English law. The words *common law* and *equity* are the best examples thereof; we have to keep the English words [. . .] because no words in French or in any other language are adequate to convey the meaning of these words, clearly linked as they are to the specific history of English law alone.[27]

Moreover, Mounin's remark quoted in note 24 on p. 16 above is a gross simplification. Legal – and other technical – registers are not wholly denotative, as he implies. Apart from the fact that even technical terms may also carry a number of connotations ('solicitor' and 'magistrate', for example, have various social connotations), such registers contain a subtle blend of technical and 'ordinary' language. Mounin himself acknowledges this in a later article: 'La "langue de droit", pour exprimer ce qu'elle a à dire, a besoin, non seulement du lexique spécifique du droit et de quelques particularités syntaxiques propres, mais de toute la langue française.'[28] Often, however, the two merge, as Alexander Lane points out:

> Le rapport entre le langage courant et le langage technique (la terminologie d'un sujet donné) est souvent difficile à déterminer. [. . .] Mais le LT a cette particularité de ne pouvoir se suffire en soi: il ne peut exister sans la base du LC. [. . .] De plus, la question de savoir si une expression donnée fait partie du LC ou du LT est également soumise à de constantes fluctuations.[29]

More concisely, Jean Darbelnet distinguishes similarly between what he calls *nomenclature* – 'les termes techniques [. . .] imposés

26. But not Scotland, which has a separate, mixed system incorporating large elements of Roman law.
27. R. David, *English Law and French Law* (Stevens & Sons and Eastern Law House, 1980), p. 39.
28. G. Mounin, 'La linguistique comme science auxiliaire dans les disciplines juridiques', *Meta*, 24 (1979), 9–17 (p. 13). It is perhaps worth noting here in passing that novices translating a legal text frequently mistake words used in an ordinary sense unfamiliar to them as being used in the legal sense of the same word. For an example, see note 26 on p. 116 below.
29. A. Lane, 'Quelques aspects de la terminologie juridique et administrative', *Babel*, 15 (1969), 31–6 (p. 32).

par le sujet' – and *vocabulaire de soutien* – 'les mots qui, étant d'une technicité moindre ou nulle, servent à actualiser les mots spécialisés et à donner ainsi au texte son organicité'.[30] But, as the qualification 'moindre ou nulle' leads one to suspect Darbelnet recognises, many words in legal usage belong neither to *langage technique* nor to *langage courant.* They are ordinary words which in technical contexts – or at the very least by association with technical contexts – have acquired an in-between status. Thus we may read in the report of an English court's judgment: 'His Lordship said it was a most anxious case.' In that sentence the word 'anxious' is a characteristically – and, indeed, in this sense almost an exclusively – legal usage (though not marked as such in the dictionaries); yet it is not a technical term or a 'term of art', as many other ordinary words have come to be when used by lawyers (e.g. 'to discharge an order', 'conveyance', 'trust', 'consideration'). In Part II attention will be confined almost wholly to proper names and terms of art properly speaking, the remaining parts of *le discours juridique* falling within the normal competence of the general translator.

It was pointed out above (on p. 10, although the term 'register' had not at that stage been introduced) that the problem can arise that there is no equivalent register in the target language. But where there is one (and that means primarily that the same 'field' exists in both cultures), it is natural and proper to use it, in so far as cultural discrepancies permit. Clearly this principle will apply to the legal systems of two major European countries like France and England. The peculiar difficulty of legal translation between English and French is, as indicated at the end of Section 1.1, that while legal registers clearly exist in English and French, just as the registers of the sciences and mathematics do, they relate to quite different systems, to two different legal worlds (unlike the scientific and mathematical registers). Let us now turn, therefore, to consider the various possible practical approaches to legal translation within the framework sketched out in this chapter.

30. J. Darbelnet, 'Réflexions sur le discours juridique', *Meta*, 24 (1979), 26–34 (p. 26).

–2–

Translation methodology

2.1 The procedures in brief

What are the practical options available to the translator faced with a 'culture-bound' source-language (SL) expression embodying a concept that has no exact equivalent in the TL? There are at most five possible procedures:[1]

(1) use a TL expression denoting the nearest equivalent concept ('county' for *département*[2]);

(2) translate word for word, making adjustments of syntax and function words if necessary ('French Academy' for *Académie française* or 'Minister for External Relations' for *Ministre des relations extérieures*);[3]

(3) borrow (i.e. adopt by transcribing) the foreign expression, adding a TL explanation (gloss) if the concept is unlikely to be familiar to the envisaged readership ('ministère public'), omitting any explanation if not ('croissant');[4] if a gloss is provided but the

1. In his recent major work *A Textbook of Translation* (Prentice Hall, 1988), p. 81, P. P. Newmark distinguishes between (general) 'methods', relating to whole texts, and (more specific) 'procedures', applicable to sentences and the smaller units of language. In terms of that distinction, the subject of this chapter is 'procedures'.

2. Since a large number of examples will be given in this chapter, the abbreviation 'e.g.' has been omitted throughout where the examples are given in brackets.

3. Strangely, P. P. Newmark, in 'Twenty-three restricted rules of translation', *Incorporated Linguist*, 12 (1973), 9–15 (p. 12), completely omits this basic method from his list of five possible techniques for translating cultural and institutional terms. In the revised and much expanded version of an earlier article (entitled 'The translation of proper names and institutional and cultural terms') which was published (under the same title) in the collection of his papers *Approaches to Translation* (Pergamon, 1981), pp. 70–83, Newmark lists (pp. 75–7) no fewer than fourteen so-called translation procedures for such terms, this time including 'literal translation'. Eight of the fourteen 'procedures', however, are not procedures in their own right at all – they are mostly special cases of other methods – and one of the eight is actually listed twice!

4. This is the process which Catford terms 'transference' – i.e. implantation of SL meaning into TL text – as distinct from translation; J. C. Catford, *A Linguistic Theory of Translation* (Oxford University Press, 1965), pp. 43–8. Newmark (who

original term is *not* transcribed, one has a straightforward paraphrase, which is essentially the same technique;[5]

(4) create a neologism, which may be:

(a) a literal translation, usually a calque (or 'loan translation'[6]), i.e. a word-for-word or morpheme-for-morpheme translation yielding either an unfamiliar but syntactically/morphologically regular combination of familiar TL words/morphemes and thus, if comprehensible, a new meaning ('university of the third age' for *université du troisième âge*, 'qualified majority' for *majorité qualifiée*, 'concertation' for *concertation*, 'francophone' for *francophone*) – what might be called a semantic calque – or else a syntactically deviant combination modelled on the pattern of the SL expression ('value-added tax' for *taxe sur la valeur ajoutée*, where one would have expected 'added-value tax'[7]) – which would be a structural calque;

(b) a naturalisation, i.e. a form of the SL expression adjusted orthographically to something nearer a TL-type form ('informatics' for *informatique*, although the English word was apparently borrowed from Russian, not French); or

(c) a wholly non-formal translation, i.e. either a purely functional equivalent ('the absolute poor' or 'the underclass' for *le quart monde*[8]) – which may come into being in the TL quite independently of the SL expression – or at least a semantic equivalent ('street furniture' for *mobilier urbain*);[9]

(5) use an existing naturalisation (which may, of course, be felt to be a native TL expression) ('department' for *département*,

---

earlier used the terms 'transliteration' and then 'transcription') now also uses this term for the process, but as a translation procedure. Since there is a possibility of confusion with the use of 'transfer' in psychology (the transfer of learned skills, etc.) and with Nida's and others' use of 'transfer' to mean a stage in the translation process, I prefer on balance to use the term 'transcription' if a technical term is required – but 'adoption', 'borrowing' or 'reproduction' are often quite adequate.

5. Newmark, *Approaches to Translation*, pp. 75–6, counts adoption coupled with transcription and adoption without it as two separate methods; paraphrase is not mentioned at all.

6. This standard term is itself a loan translation – of the German *Lehnübersetzung*. Oddly, Newmark, *Approaches to Translation*, p. 179, wants to replace it by the even longer and less transparent term 'through-translation'.

7. As late as 1962 the French term was still rendered as '= purchase tax' in the third edition of the *Supplement* (Harrap, 1962) to Part One (*French–English*) of *Harrap's Standard French and English Dictionary*.

8. In the sociological sense of 'sub-proletariat in the rich industrialised nations'.

9. Obviously a concept which both is absolutely new and is exclusive to the SL culture (or, at any rate, unknown to the TL culture) cannot strictly have a *functional* equivalent.

'naivety' for *naïveté*). This technique is not to be confused with the often unconscious use of an existing TL form in the hitherto non-TL sense of a cognate SL form – which is a type of calque: in our context a (semantic) Gallicism, or French meaning in English clothing, as in 'sympathetic' for *sympathique*.

Before we look at each of these in a little more detail – their nature and relative advantages and drawbacks – it is worth emphasising at the outset that, more particularly where culture-specific texts are concerned, the techniques and style of translation chosen must always depend in large measure on the translation's purpose and readership.[10] Attention will be directed to this at appropriate points in the sections which follow.

2.2 Functional equivalence

Using a TL expression which denotes the nearest equivalent concept is the method of *functional* (contextual, cultural) *equivalence* (which is what Nida and Taber appear to mean by 'dynamic equivalence'[11]) as opposed to purely semantic or formal equivalence. It disregards formal correspondence between SL and TL and, in that it entails reference to a wholly native TL concept (institution, activity, person), will invariably be the most idiomatic and natural-looking rendering. A further example would be 'the Cabinet' for *le Conseil des ministres* (not to be translated as 'the Council of Ministers', which (a) corresponds to nothing in British culture[12] and (b) is the title in English of the decision-making body of the European Community). Even where, then, as in the legal field, concepts differ between cultures, it is generally permissible to use the nearest equivalent term. We know that breakfast in France is not at all the same as breakfast in England, but it is none the less inconceivable that *petit déjeuner* should be translated as anything other than '(Continental) breakfast'.

But how near – functionally and connotatively (say, in terms of social prestige) – does the TL referent have to be to the SL referent

10. One of the few writers this century to have taken due account of this vital fact in his theorising is Theodore Savory: see his excellent book *The Art of Translation*, 2nd edn (Cape, 1968), esp. pp. 18 and 57–9.

11. E. A. Nida and C. R. Taber, *The Theory and Practice of Translation* (Brill, 1969, repr. 1974), esp. p. 14.

12. Throughout this book it will be assumed that texts are being translated primarily for the British reader of English (or, at any rate, the reader familiar with British English and institutions) and for English lawyers rather than ones from other common-law jurisdictions.

for the use of its linguistic label to be acceptable as a translation of the SL label? Obviously, this must to a large extent be a matter for the translator's judgment and discretion according to his knowledge of the cultural background and of the features of the referents concerned.[13] Sometimes an SL expression will appear to combine some of the features of two TL functional equivalents: thus *recteur d'académie* corresponds partly to 'vice-chancellor' and partly to 'chief education officer' or 'director of education'. In such cases, one would choose whichever TL expression best suited the context, and that decision would not strictly be a linguistic one, as it would depend on a knowledge of the world rather than on knowledge of the SL or the TL. As a general guide, however, it should be borne in mind that the more popular the nature of the text and of its readership, the less need there is for strict functional equivalence; thus 'county' might do as a rendering of *département* in a newspaper report – but not in a specialist document or book on local government in France, where accuracy of reference would be important. On the other hand, 'Cabinet' really is the only possible translation of *Conseil des ministres* in any circumstances: if the context is such that the differences between the French and British bodies are misleadingly great, then the only course is to leave *Conseil des ministres* untranslated and reproduce it, inserting the necessary explanations at the appropriate point or points in the text.

In a good many cases the functionally or contextually equivalent translation will be mandatory. This is true particularly of non-culture-specific public notices and the like: thus, although *défense d'entrer* could be 'No entry', 'No admittance', 'No access', 'Keep out' or 'Private' according to context, *défense de fumer* admits of no alternative to 'No smoking'. But legal examples are not far to seek either: *Grands arrêts* as a book title, say, would almost certainly have to be 'Leading Cases' and *Chronique des tribunaux* in a newspaper might well have to be 'Law Report'.[14]

Conversely, there is one case where the functionally equivalent TL term cannot be used. This is where the referent of the TL term – usually an institution or an office – is peculiar to the TL culture, e.g. 'the Master of the Rolls' or 'the Treasury'. The latter term (or 'the Exchequer') should not be used to translate *le ministère des Finances*

13. An excellent account of the main factors which have to be considered in the legal field is given in Susan Šarčević's article 'Conceptual Dictionaries for Translation in the Field of Law', *International Journal of Lexicography*, 2 (1989), 277–93.

14. It is worth pointing out in passing that, as in these examples, a functional or contextual equivalent may in fact not be a translation – in the sense of a semantic equivalent – at all. Another example would be the warning on food packaging: 'Best before . . .' versus *A consommer de préférence avant. . .*

because of the risk of confusion – at least in some cases – with the actual British institution (and it must accordingly be translated word for word as 'the Ministry of Finance'). Attention has been drawn to this particular pitfall before – notably by Newmark.[15] But nowhere does anyone appear to have enunciated the criterion by which the translator may decide whether a term peculiar to the TL culture is or is not an admissible translation. The omission is the more curious – and serious – as the problem confronts translators quite regularly. Not all terms peculiar to the TL culture need to be rejected as potentially misleading. After all, in many contexts 'county' *is* an acceptable translation of *département*, although counties (rendered in French by *comtés*) are, strictly, unique to the United Kingdom as administrative units in terms of their rôle, powers, etc. Somehow, then, a line has to be drawn between such acceptable culture-specific functional equivalents and those which are unacceptable ('Master of the Rolls' for *premier président de la cour d'appel*).

The distinction to be observed is quite simply the one between generic and specific, and the practical test to be applied is whether the indefinite article may be used in front of the TL term or not: thus 'a county', 'a barrister', 'a court of appeal', but not (normally) 'a Master of the Rolls', 'a House of Lords'. The first three terms are generic and therefore usable, the latter two are specific and therefore not usable, as translations. (Even generics will not all be acceptable as translations, however, as some will still be too culture-bound – 'recorder' to denote a judicial post, for example. But such terms will probably only rarely be the functional equivalents of SL terms in any case.) In many cases of doubt – e.g. 'Lord Chancellor', 'Foreign Secretary' – the availability of clearly generic alternatives will usually enable the difficulty to be circumvented (use 'Minister of Justice', 'Minister for Foreign Affairs'); while in others one can either rely on context to make it clear that the reference is not to the British institution (e.g. 'High Court' is just about acceptable as a rendering of *tribunal de grande instance* in a translation intended for the general reader) or else consider that the degree of functional equivalence is not sufficient to justify using the TL term anyway ('High Court' not acceptable for *tribunal de grande instance* in a specialist text – see p. 75 below).

Generally speaking, the technique of using a functional equivalent may be regarded as the *ideal* method of translation.

15. P. P. Newmark, 'The translation of proper names and institutional and cultural terms', esp. original version, *Incorporated Linguist*, 16 (1977), 59–63 (pp. 60 and 62).

2.3 Word-for-word translation

Word-for-word translation (which is usually what is meant by 'literal translation'[16]) is the method of *formal* (lexical) *equivalence* (at the level of either the word or higher units). It disregards the collocation of the words, the syntagmatic relations between them which normally determine how the individual words will be rendered (if at all) in a given context. Thus *conseil* = 'council' and *ministres* = 'ministers', but *Conseil des ministres* = 'Cabinet' (functional equivalence), whereas the method of literal translation, ignoring the effect of the collocation, would produce 'Council of Ministers' (only semantic equivalence).

During the course of the twentieth century, critical opinion has swung markedly away from acceptance of literal translation (i.e. conveying the form of the original as well as the content) as an aim and has come down firmly in favour of functional equivalence (conveying primarily the ideas of the original) as the goal to be attained – often expressed as 'achieving the same effect on the TL reader as the SL text has on the SL reader' or else as 'using the words the author would have used had he been writing in the TL'.[17]

This critical trend, by and large, seems wholly defensible seeing that the translator's paramount duty – in the expression stage of translation – is to write a natural, idiomatic form of the TL, whereas so many practitioners of the art, especially beginners, adhere slavishly to the words of the original even when doing so produces a quite unnatural effect in the TL. It nevertheless remains true that there are circumstances in which a word-for-word trans-

16. Some writers, however, including Newmark, have distinguished between 'literal' translation, in which any necessary adjustments are made in order to comply with TL grammar (the sense in which I use both terms interchangeably), and 'word-for-word' translation, in which they are not (so that, say, 'Le Conseil des ministres se réunit le mercredi' would translate word for word as 'The Council of the Ministers itself reunites the Wednesday'). That example suffices to show that for the practical purposes of producing finished translation in the real world the latter type of translation can be ignored.

17. This approach would seem logically to entail the strictly impossible task of translating a fourteenth-century text into the fourteenth-century form of the TL – a point conveniently passed over in silence by its advocates; but the flaw can be largely eliminated by stressing that the effect to be produced on the TL reader is that made by the SL text on its original readers *when it was first written*. On the other hand, this formulation still does not make it possible to use the words the (fourteenth-century) author would have used in the (fourteenth-century) TL, and the impossibility of producing an effect on a twentieth-century TL reader equivalent to that of a fourteenth-century SL text on a twentieth-century SL reader has to be conceded.

lation is actually mandatory: namely, whenever such a translation happens to represent the nearest functional equivalent in the TL culture. Thus, for example, 'court of appeal' (usually without capitals, since there is more than one in France – see Section 6.5) is the ideal and, indeed, the only possible translation of *cour d'appel*. This is, in fact, a particular manifestation of the general principle that word-for-word translations, *so long as they are natural in the target language*, should not be shunned merely because they *are* literal translations. As Newmark puts it, 'a good translator abandons a literal version only when it is plainly inexact or [. . .] badly written. A bad translator will always do his best to avoid translating word for word';[18] and he is right to have pointed out – for example in his extended review of Delisle's *L'Analyse du discours*[19] – that the Paris School theorists led by Seleskovitch have taken their enthusiasm for functionally equivalent translation too far.

Word-for-word translation, then, will frequently be the best, and it can be divided into the following four categories. A formal translation will either

(a) as we have seen, represent the same – or most nearly the same ('Prime Minister' for *premier ministre*) – concept as the TL term; or
(b) represent a different concept and either not correspond functionally at all or else not do so as closely as an alternative, non-literal translation – in other words will be a *faux ami* – 'common law' for *droit commun* (= 'ordinary law'), 'magistrate' for *magistrat* (for which see Section 7.2); or
(c) not correspond to any concept familiar in the TL culture but be semantically equivalent and fairly transparent in its general meaning ('National Assembly' for *Assemblée nationale*, 'Court of Cassation' for *Cour de cassation*); or
(d) lack any obvious meaning altogether, possibly even to the point of appearing ridiculous ('Council of State' for *Conseil d'État*, 'public ministry' for *ministère public* or 'Keeper of the Seals' for *Garde des Sceaux* – *not* a zoological official!).

Only literal translations falling into categories (a) and (c) are likely to be acceptable – indeed, those in (a) are invariably mandatory. Those in categories (b) and (d) will usually be unacceptable, though there will be many borderline cases, as each individual translator

18. Newmark, *A Textbook of Translation*, p. 76.
19. P. P. Newmark, 'Jean Delisle's theory of translation', *Incorporated Linguist*, 22 (1983), 136–8.

must decide for himself whether or not the meaning of a literal translation is either close enough to the SL concept or else sufficiently transparent in its unfamiliar meaning, as the case may be.

In that it is more or less mechanical and straightforward while yet often yielding the right result, word-for-word translation may be regarded as the *basic* method.

Failing the methods of either functional or formal equivalence (or both combined), the next alternative is to adopt (transcribe) the original SL expression.

2.4 Transcription

Inevitably (cf. Section 1.1), there will be a number of SL expressions which defy translation in the strict, narrow sense because nothing truly comparable to the corresponding concept exists in the TL culture and a literal translation makes no sense. The alternative of reproducing the SL expression with or without a gloss, or else paraphrasing it, is essentially a *pis aller* – it admits defeat.[20]

Whether one transcribes or paraphrases, whether one glosses a transcription or not, and the length of any gloss or paraphrase[21] will all depend on the nature of the text and its readership (learned or popular).

There are two customary ways of transcribing and glossing. The SL term may be reproduced, conventionally (but not, for clarity's sake, in this book) in italics or between inverted commas, and followed in brackets by the TL gloss, e.g. 'auditeur (junior member of the Conseil d'État)'; in which case subsequent reference will be by means of the SL term ('auditeur'), the translator relying on the reader's memory for the definition. Conversely, the gloss may be incorporated into the text, with the SL term being given in brackets after the first mention, again usually in italics or between inverted commas, e.g. 'the junior members of the Conseil d'État (the auditeurs)'; in which case subsequent reference will normally be by means of the gloss (or paraphrase: but either will have to be short),

20. It is therefore curious to find Newmark describing this method, for whatever reason, as 'the basic method' in his 'The translation of proper names', in *Approaches to Translation*, p. 75. In his more recent *A Textbook of Translation*, p. 70, however, he states that he believes literal translation 'to be the basic translation procedure'.

21. I can see no useful distinction to be made in this context between 'gloss' and 'paraphrase'; but, in line with what was said in Section 1.1, a gloss generally tends to accompany that which it explains, and I have accordingly used 'paraphrase' to refer to explanations *not* accompanied by the SL terms they explain. Both glosses and paraphrases are in the nature of explanations or definitions.

the translator judging that the original SL term is of no interest, or at any rate importance, to the TL reader. The former procedure will be more appropriate in learned material, where specialist readers may have some knowledge of the relevant area of the SL culture; while the latter method of presentation (or plain paraphrase) will be better if the text is general rather than technical in nature and/or if the readership is non-specialist.

In the case of a specialist readership it may sometimes be desirable to mention the SL term in brackets – or even adopt it throughout – even where an acceptable functionally equivalent and/or word-for-word translation is available, rather than rely on the transparency of the latter's reference to ensure that the reader knows precisely which body, office, etc., is being discussed. But generally if the need for such a safety device is felt, it suggests that a chosen word-for-word translation is not in fact transparent enough in meaning to be acceptable; a functionally equivalent TL term, such as 'industrial tribunal' for *conseil de prud'hommes*, however, should in principle always be sufficiently close to the SL term's meaning to obviate the need for any mention of the SL term. But the fact remains that specialists may need to know the SL designation for one reason or another (e.g. the SL title of a series of law reports, in order to be able to find, and perhaps have translated, the report of a cited case). The only other reason for unnecessarily introducing transcriptions of SL terms into a translation – to provide atmosphere and local colour ('He lit another Gauloise') – is unlikely to apply to legal texts other than, say, passages relating to lawyers and the law in Balzac or other novelists.

There is, however, one special instance of SL-term transcription which should be mentioned even though it likewise does not occur very often in legal texts, namely acronyms and similar abbreviations – i.e. words or abbreviations formed from the initial letters of other words, usually constituting the names of official or commercial bodies. Since such abbreviations are in the nature of names, they do not have full meaning in the normal sense and are clearly untranslatable. Consequently, either their full form must be discovered (if the translator can ascertain it – no easy task sometimes!) and translated in whatever is the most appropriate manner, or else – a better method, as it is more economical of space and reflects the fact that most such abbreviations have no meaning to translate – they must be retained and transcribed, with a gloss or translation of their expanded form in brackets following their first mention. Alternatively, the initials of the TL gloss or translation may occasionally be substituted ('CCP' for *CPP = Code de procédure pénale*/'Code of Criminal Procedure').[22] In legal contexts acronyms and abbreviations are likely to be confined to those of associations and companies, etc., appearing as litigants and to codes, law reports and other publications – such as the *JO* (*Journal officiel* – France's official gazette) – where the possible need to consult the documents in question makes it the more imperative to retain the SL abbreviation if the expanded SL form is not given anywhere in the translation.

Lastly, in rare instances, usually euphemistic or ideological in nature, a combination of the transcription method and word-for-word translation may be called for. Thus *les événements de mai 1968* might become 'les événements de mai 1968 – the "events" of May 1968 (i.e. the student uprising)'.

2.5 Neologism

Less needs to be said about creating neologisms. Concepts which are new (or at least new or foreign to the TL culture) are likely to require new TL words to label them sooner or later, though this is not inevitable – old words may be combined to form new compounds or phrases, for example ('third world' for *tiers monde*); and translators should generally refrain from creating neologisms.

The mandatory test is that of necessity: it is no business of the translator's to create a new word or expression if the SL expression can be adequately and conveniently translated by one of the methods already described. Creating a neologism should be a last resort. Indeed, a neologism is rarely as satisfactory as any other method of translation, because it will generally have to be glossed for the benefit of the TL reader in any case when it is first used, so the original expression might as well be transcribed and glossed. Since any SL term invariably *can* be rendered by transcribing and glossing, the only situation in which a neologism is justified is one where not only the condition of real need for it is met but also the translator deliberately wants to establish an expression for the SL concept in the TL because, on a long-term view, the concept in question is clearly of an importance widely transcending the SL

22. In this connection, it should be noted that most of the major international organisations have a different abbreviation/acronym for each of their official languages, e.g. *OMS* = WHO, *OTAN* = NATO, *CEE* = EEC, so obviously such abbreviations – which may be acronyms in one language but not, in the strict sense of forming a pronounceable word, in the other, as in the case of *ONU* = UN – must be 'translated', i.e. replaced by their official equivalent.

culture (or at least of evident importance to the TL culture). Neologisms must not be created by default – through laziness or inadvertence.

It is worth noting, therefore, that of the nine examples given in Section 2.1, (4) (a–c), only the functionally/semantically equivalent ones ('the absolute poor', 'the underclass', 'street furniture') are acceptable (on the assumption, in the case of *quart monde*, that 'fourth world' is reserved for the geopolitical sense of the very poorest countries of the world). The remainder manifestly fail the test of necessity: *université du troisième âge* could perfectly well be rendered in a number of semantically equivalent ways, such as 'Senior Citizens' University' or 'university for the retired' ('university of the third age' does not even have the merit of being comprehensible); 'qualified majority' – an expression open to any number of interpretations, given the polysemy of 'qualified' – appears to mask a meaning that could be plainly conveyed by '(specified) special majority'; 'concertation' seems to have no meaning not already covered by 'coordination', 'consultation' or 'acting in concert'; 'francophone' is a completely redundant synonym of 'French-speaking'; 'value-added tax' (which we are now saddled with, of course: this is precisely the danger – as with 'qualified majority'[23]) should have been 'added-value tax'; and 'informatics' appears to mean nothing different from the existing term 'information science'. All these neologisms could be described as (formal) Gallicisms or English in Frenchified clothing (see Section 2.6).

In conclusion, any neologism that is created should also satisfy the requirements of naturalness (conformity with regular TL grammatical, morphological and phonological patterns, etc.[24]) and economy (a succinct neologism being ultimately preferable to a long-winded paraphrase – and transcription of the original similarly

23. Cf. J.-P. Vinay and J. Darbelnet, *Stylistique comparée du français et de l'anglais* (Didier, 1958, repr. 1977), pp. 53–4: 'Nous touchons là un problème extrêmement grave [. . .] celui des changements intellectuels, culturels et linguistiques que peut entraîner à la longue l'existence de documents importants [. . .] rédigés par des traducteurs qui ne peuvent ou n'osent pas s'aventurer dans les traductions obliques. A une époque où la centralisation excessive et le manque de respect pour la culture d'autrui poussent les organisations internationales à adopter une langue de travail unique pour rédiger des textes qui sont ensuite traduits hâtivement par des traducteurs mal considérés et trop peu nombreux, on peut craindre de voir les quatre-cinquièmes du globe se nourrir exclusivement de traductions et périr intellectuellement de ce régime de bouillie pour les chats.'

24. Including phonological distinctness: the neologism 'compunication' no doubt failed to catch on primarily because it was in practice indistinguishable auditorily from 'communication'.

better than a longer neologism). Examples from the legal field which fulfil these further requirements satisfactorily are 'decriminalisation' for *décriminalisation* (a morpheme-for-morpheme calque) and 'continuing-effect clause' for *clause de rémanence*, in international investment treaties (a functional equivalent).

2.6 Naturalisation

Least of all need be said about the use of an existing TL naturalisation – for two reasons. Firstly, it is a special case of word-for-word translation (or of borrowing) and of neologism, from which it is therefore only doubtfully separable as a category; and secondly, that being so, an established naturalisation can be regarded as a legitimate standard translation.

In practice, the only case where the translator needs to be especially vigilant is that of proper names. Some SL names may not be immediately recognised if they are themselves naturalisations or calques of foreign names (*Plaisance*, the French calque for Piacenza); while others may have naturalised TL forms (Rheims, Lyons, Marseilles) which are showing signs of dying out and being replaced, graphically at least, by the SL forms. (Indeed, among French place-names, only Dunkirk seems to be determinedly defying this trend – appropriately enough, and no doubt precisely because of its Second-World-War associations and its consequent allusive use as a common noun or as an adjective: 'Dunkirk spirit', etc.).

A long-standing naturalisation in the legal field is 'cassation'.[25]

2.7 Choice of procedure and consistency

Disregarding naturalisation, then, for the reasons just given, one may make the following general comments by way of recapitulating the remaining four methods of translation.

Of these methods, transcription (borrowing) is arguably not strictly translation at all but an alternative way of dealing with culture-specific terms when translation in the narrower sense is not possible. Paraphrase is vulnerable to the same objection, and that in itself justifies its being classed with transcription as one and the same method – a method which is, generally speaking, an admis-

25. Going back to the fifteenth century, according to *The Oxford English Dictionary* and *The Oxford Dictionary of English Etymology*.

sion of defeat. It is, none the less, still marginally preferable to neologising, since a neologism not only to some extent admits defeat but also actually tampers with the TL, following the reasoning that if one is not ingenious enough to find a ready-made translation, one must invent one; and that is not a very good principle to follow. Both these methods – transcription and neologism – are subordinate to the two standard methods of functional or semantic equivalence and literal translation.

On general linguistic grounds, therefore, the precise order of precedence of the various methods is the following:

(1) word-for-word translation if this yields a functional equivalent;
(2) a non-literal translation representing a functional equivalent in the TL;
(3) a word-for-word or non-literal translation that represents a semantic equivalent but is not the label of a functionally equivalent referent (institution, office, etc.) in the TL culture (because there is none);
(4) transcription (sometimes necessary in any case for the benefit of specialist readers); and
(5) neologism.

Often, of course, there will in practice be a choice between different acceptable TL versions (of the same SL expression) yielded by more than one of the methods (as well as a choice of whether or not to gloss if the transcription method is adopted). In such cases, other factors determining the ultimate choice have to be considered. A transcription or a neologism without any gloss may simply not be understood. Using a TL term representing a functional equivalent (which, in the nature of things, will never be absolutely identical in all its attributes) may mislead the reader unfamiliar with the SL culture.

This brings us back once again to the readership and purpose of the translation, which are, as was suggested at the end of Section 2.1, the key non-linguistic factors affecting the translator's choice of translation technique and style. How well informed is the reader about the SL culture in general and the text's subject-matter in particular? Does the translation have any aesthetic pretensions or is its purpose purely informative? If the reader is not familiar with the SL culture and is relying on the translation to inform him, how detailed and accurate does this information need to be? And so on. These are questions that fall to be considered as we approach the more strictly practical aspects of this study.

But as the focus shifts from the primarily linguistic to the predominantly legal part of the book, a word should be said about the relevance and relative weight of linguistic and non-linguistic criteria in the translation of specialised texts such as legal documents. At different points in the process, as we have seen, linguistic and extra-linguistic considerations will have priority or at least come into play and be decisive.

It follows from what has been said so far in this section that not all culture-specific terms in a single text can be translated consistently, i.e. consistently in method, by using the same technique for each. Indeed, it will not usually be possible even to translate consistently all the members of a set of terms in a given semantic field. Thus, taking the organisation of the French courts as an example, while *Cour de cassation* can be rendered (word for word) as 'Court of Cassation', *Conseil d'État* must be transcribed, and *tribunal paritaire des baux ruraux* is probably best translated by the functional equivalent 'agricultural land tribunal'. Here the linguistic constraints must override the desire for consistency, which must not be achieved at the expense of intelligibility. On the other hand, in a simple *list* of, say, French courts (to continue with the same example) such inconsistency might appear unacceptably incongruous and a compromise would then have to be effected, either by transcribing all the names or, if there was a need but no space to gloss, by translating them all using a mixture of word-for-word translations and functional equivalents as appropriate (whereby *Conseil d'État* would become 'Council of State').

The linguistic impossibility of translating institutional terms properly using a single method consistently throughout a given text has to be recognised and conceded – and may seem to a lawyer singularly inconvenient in the field of law. But the consistency rightly striven for by lawyers is not of the same kind: it is, rather, on the one hand, a consistency in applying the law (which is not a linguistic matter and only affects translation – indirectly – in bilingual communities like Canada, where obviously there must be consistency between the French and English versions of legislation if statutes are to be applied consistently by the courts) and, on the other, consistency of reference of terms used within a given text. The latter is certainly a linguistic matter and it means in practical terms that, particularly in statutes and regulations, the same SL term or expression should consistently be rendered by the same TL term or expression (irrespective of translation method chosen). This presents no particular problem for the translator, who must simply bear the principle in mind and be sure to refrain from varying the terminology for purely stylistic reasons (what Fowler in his *Dictionary of Modern English Usage* calls 'elegant variation'): consistency of reference is paramount, and the reader must be able to be sure that a repetition of a term refers to the same thing as the term did when it was used before, while use of a different term betokens a different referent. Thus, if at the outset of a text the translator decides to translate *contravention* as 'petty offence' rather than, say, 'minor offence', he must not subsequently use 'minor offence' to render *contravention*, since otherwise the reader will wonder whether some other category of offence is being referred to. (To this end, it is advisable in long texts for the translator to keep a note of the renderings used of key terms as he goes along.)

This does not of course mean that the same SL word in *different collocations and contexts* will have to be translated by the same TL word each time, for that again is a purely linguistic matter, where linguistic constraints must prevail. To take the example of the word *conseil*, while 'Constitutional Council' may be an acceptable translation of *Conseil constitutionnel*, *Conseil des ministres* must be rendered as 'Cabinet' and *Conseil d'État* will be transcribed as it is. Even where one and the same SL term is used repeatedly in the same text, the translator must be allowed some discretion to vary his translation of it. It may sometimes be helpful to render it in two or more different ways: thus *ordre juridique* will often be translated as 'legal system' when referring to an individual country, but might be better rendered as 'legal order' when used of, say, European Community law or in more philosophical or abstract contexts. Similarly, *privation de liberté* will in some semantic contexts within a given text be more neatly and naturally rendered by 'imprisonment' than by the more general, abstract 'deprivation/loss of liberty'.

What the lawyer can reasonably (and usually will) insist on is that, having once decided on linguistic grounds that, say, *Conseil constitutionnel* is best translated as 'Constitutional Council', the translator must adhere to that translation throughout the text; and that, correspondingly, any reference to 'the Council' will likewise mean the *Conseil constitutionnel* unless there is an indication to the contrary.[26] Subject to that requirement and to the possibility that

26. Note, however, that French lawyers – no doubt under the influence of the principle of literary style, taught in schools, that synonyms should continually be used to avoid repetition of words – are less rigid about this requirement than English ones: 'That in the same law or contract the same words should be used in two

recognised or established or 'official' translations of certain terms exist, the translator must be free to use the various translation techniques as he professionally judges best, simply to ensure that the translation makes good sense and reads well in the TL. It is probably unnecessary to add, finally, that for reasons of clarity in the presentation of the French legal system in Part II it will naturally be impossible to group the legal terms together according to the method by which they may best be translated.

---

senses, or that different words should be used for the same idea, is not to them a matter of great reproach, provided the sense is clear'; Sir Maurice Amos and F. P. Walton, *An Introduction to French Law*, 3rd edn by F. H. Lawson, A. E. Anton and L. N. Brown (Oxford University Press, 1967), p. 16.

–3–

The business of legal translation

3.1 The background

Obviously, in one place or another, legal translation covers the written part of all aspects of the law; and, equally obviously, it would not be possible to deal with every sphere of the law in a book of this size. For the purposes of this study, therefore, I shall be assuming a background of translating many of the documents used or produced by international organisations – including international courts – working in (at least) English and French.

Such documents may comprise agendas, minutes, reports, background documents and research papers needed for the meetings of committees dealing with a wide range of legal fields and issues; the successive drafts of international conventions; surveys of national legislation in all fields; written pleadings and oral addresses setting out issues of fact and law in cases before international courts, often referring in detail to proceedings in national courts; and the judgments of international courts. In other words, texts for whose translation a knowledge of different systems, procedures, institutions and office-holders is more important than a knowledge of substantive law – and it is perhaps surprising to discover in just how many texts this is the case. The translation of material such as contracts and legislation (other than extracts from national legislation needed purely for information purposes) is not specifically covered in this book, whose main concern is to introduce the reader to the French legal *system*.

As has already been pointed out, the readership of any translation is a very important – if often overlooked – factor influencing the choice of translation method. From the translator's point of view, what matters most is that the readers of such texts will probably have specialist knowledge of the law and legal systems of their own countries but usually little or no familiarity with foreign legal systems, legal training having been notoriously parochial in this respect hitherto. This is especially true of English readers, as the English legal profession has remained until quite recent times (effectively Britain's entry into the Common Market) more than usually closed to the legal world outside its own and other common-law jurisdictions – a world including, of course, most of Europe.

A further vital feature of the readership of the types of text just described is that the readers of an English translation are more likely to be non-native than native speakers of English, e.g. Austrians or Norwegians, and thus have little knowledge of the common-law terminology of the English legal system, though they may well be broadly familiar with the French civil-law system. The problem thus arises that for, say, a German, English will usually be easier to read than French but French legal procedures and institutions easier to understand than English ones.

In sum, what Newmark says of translating institutional terms in general will apply: 'We may assume the stress in the text is on SL institutions and [. . .] culture rather than the TL [. . .] and that the reader of the translation is not as well-informed as the reader of the original.'[1]

Bearing in mind all the foregoing and that the greater the degree of technicality of any term, the smaller the practical possibility of actually translating it (i.e. finding an equivalent TL term) at all, I have selected for consideration in Part II the most general facets of the law: its branches, the various forms of legislation, the courts, the legal professions and criminal procedure and penalties. These are all reasonably accessible to the non-lawyer and are areas where the differences between the English and French systems are obvious and/or important, yet which, while posing problems of a methodological nature and containing pitfalls for the unwary or legally naïve translator, offer at least some scope for elucidation and satisfactory translation within acceptable limits of accuracy.

The sort of legal translation envisaged in this book having thus been indicated, a brief word should now be said about two potential sources of practical assistance: the terminology employed in English-speaking (or French- and English-speaking) civil-law jurisdictions; and bilingual or multilingual legal dictionaries.

3.2 English-speaking or bilingual civil-law jurisdictions

The seemingly obvious major example of a bilingual civil-law jurisdiction is the Canadian province of Quebec. To say, however,

1. P. P. Newmark, 'The translation of proper names and institutional and cultural terms', *Incorporated Linguist*, 16 (1977), 59–63 (p. 61).

that Quebec is a civil-law jurisdiction is a gross simplification. Already in 1764, a year after the cession of Canada to Great Britain by France, an ordinance established a judicial system on English lines, the judges to determine agreeably to equity, having nevertheless regard to the laws of England so far as circumstances permitted. This resulted in the continued application of French civil law in disputes between French-speaking Canadians. The Quebec Act of 1774 provided for the application of the criminal law of England in Quebec, while affirming that in all matters of controversy relating to civil rights and property resort was to be had to French law; and in 1866 a bilingual Civil Code based on the *Code Napoléon* was adopted, although here too English law was – and has remained – influential. When those parts of the Code which were drafted in French were at the time translated into English, a new civil-law vocabulary had to be devised, but for some reason common-law terms which would have been suitable as equivalents were not used. Many of the English terms are as a result, and however incredibly, almost meaningless word-for-word translations of the French – and have often been reproduced in subsequent statutes (for the sake of consistency and to avoid causing confusion by using different terms for a single concept; cf. what was said on pp. 32–33 above). To take but one example, *rente* ('annuity') is translated as 'rent'. Nor, likewise, was the opportunity taken to correct such renderings in the new Draft Civil Code submitted to the Government in 1977 and being enacted in stages. It is thus laid down, for example, that 'Marriage is proved by an act of marriage' (i.e. a marriage certificate)! Finally, unlike the rest of Canada, Quebec retains two separate legal professions – but those of *avocat* ('advocate' or 'lawyer', there being no official translation) and *notaire* ('notary') on the French model, not barrister and solicitor. On the other hand, there is no *parquet* or *ministère public* on the French pattern (see Section 7.2).

In sum, then, Quebec has a mixed system rather than a clear-cut civil-law one. Indeed, it has been pointed out that 'le système en vigueur au Québec, façonné par les institutions parlementaires et le droit britanniques, présente moins de ressemblances que de différences avec la famille romano-germanique'.[2] Clearly a study of the legal system of Quebec is unlikely to prove very helpful for translating terms from the French legal system – and the same is true of the American state of Louisiana, which also has a mixed system.

2. Jean-Claude Gémar, 'La traduction juridique et son enseignement: aspects théoriques et pratiques', *Meta*, 24 (1979), 35–53 (p. 49).

More promising at first sight are the jurisdictions of the Indian Ocean islands of Mauritius and Seychelles. The official language of Mauritius is English, while in Seychelles both English and French are official languages, but English is the language of administration and the law. In both cases, however, the legal system is again a mixed one. The basis is of French substantive law: thus the 1804 *Code civil* was applied in Mauritius from 1805 and is still in force; in Seychelles it was introduced in 1805 but has since been replaced by a new Civil Code (1976). The basis of French law is overlaid by a system of courts and procedures modelled on the English system. Xavier Blanc-Jouvan describes the Mauritian system as 'une sorte de synthèse entre deux systèmes qui s'opposent diamétralement [. . .]: le système français et le système anglais'.[3] In both jurisdictions judges, magistrates and practising lawyers are normally trained in the common law and qualify as barristers in England or elsewhere. At the same time, there are in both islands French-style notaries, who in Seychelles can combine their office with that of an attorney (the local equivalent of a solicitor). Once trained, these practitioners return to the islands and apply what is essentially French law, interpreted in the light of French case-law.

Since our concern in this guide is primarily with the French legal system rather than with French substantive law (and it is precisely the system which is modelled on the English one in both islands), the jurisdictions of Mauritius and Seychelles will likewise not help us very much. Allusion will, however, be made to the Mauritian system again in Chapter 7.

Mention should be made, lastly, of a mixed system nearer home, namely the Scottish legal system. For historical reasons Scotland, although part of the United Kingdom, has a legal system distinct from that of England and Wales, with separate hierarchies of courts and judges; a separate legal profession with different training and qualifications; different procedures and terminology; and, on most topics, separate bodies of substantive law too. Until the nineteenth century, Roman law was the most powerful single external influence, and the result is that the Scottish legal system stands midway between a civil-law and a common-law one.

From the point of view of this book, therefore, Scotland too is of only minor, peripheral interest – in this case because the system has not undergone any influence by the French legal system specifically

3. X. Blanc-Jouvan, 'Introduction à l'étude comparée des Droits de l'Océan Indien', in *Études de droit privé français et mauricien* (Presses Universitaires de France, 1969), 19–33 (p. 31).

and it consequently shares few of the latter's institutions. Furthermore, although the language of the Scottish system is undoubtedly English, where it differs from the terminology used in England and Wales it would tend not to be regarded as 'standard' English legal terminology, in much the same way as Scotticisms in general (e.g. 'outwith') are not regarded as standard English. (It should perhaps be pointed out also that the Scottish legal system is in fact integrated into the English one to the extent (only) that final appeal lies in civil – but not criminal – cases to the House of Lords, whose judgments in Scottish cases are binding on Scottish courts.[4])

There is, however, in Scotland a system of public prosecution analogous to the *ministère public* in France (as now in England also), and reference will accordingly be made to Scottish terminology as well as Mauritian in Chapter 7.

3.3 Dictionaries

A much more useful source of aid in translating French legal terms is provided by bilingual dictionaries, although these are frequently disappointing and not as helpful as the novice might expect. The situation has been neatly summarised by Jean-Claude Gémar:

> Tous les auteurs [. . .] signalent invariablement l'absence d'une tentative concertée de lexicographie juridique 'différentielle' qui tiendrait compte à la fois de la réalité juridique et des impératifs linguistiques.
>
> La production dans ce domaine est faible. Le traducteur se trouve soit en présence de (bons mais rares) dictionnaires juridiques unilingues [. . .] soit en présence de dictionnaires de traduction bilingues, les meilleurs généralement, ou multilingues, les plus faibles et les moins fiables.[5]

With the exception of the French–English–German volume of Herbst and Readett's three-volume English/French/German dictionary, which is the largest and most comprehensive available in the field (although by no means reliable), and O'Rooney's glossary (discussed below), the multilingual dictionaries are indeed so bad that they have not been consulted for the purposes of this study. A detailed review of the available bilingual dictionaries would be out of place here, but a few comments may be offered on one or two of the more useful ones.

4. Although there are always at least two Scottish Law Lords (who customarily sit in Scottish appeals), Professor Walker in his *Oxford Companion to Law* (Clarendon Press, 1980), p. 1111, describes this as 'still mainly an appeal to foreign lawyers'.

5. Gémar, 'La traduction juridique', p. 49.

The least unsatisfactory of the modern bilingual dictionaries commercially available hitherto has probably been Michel Doucet's French–English/English–French *Dictionnaire juridique et économique. Legal and Economic Dictionary* (La Maison du Dictionnaire, 1979), but it is full of mistakes (and misprints) none the less. Curiously, the French–English section contains substantially more pages than the English–French part, and the French–English/English–French *Dictionnaire économique et juridique* by J. Baleyte and others (Éditions de Navarre, 1989) is probably more useful for translation from English into French, as the reverse proportions apply in its case; but it is correspondingly less useful for translation into English. Like so many technical dictionaries, Doucet, Herbst and Readett, and Baleyte all include entries for large numbers of non-technical words which have no place in such works, so that the dictionaries are effectively smaller than they appear to be. Conversely, the French–English part of *Harrap's New Standard French and English Dictionary*, which makes no claim to be a technical dictionary, contains translations of many legal terms (including a fair number not to be found in the legal dictionaries), and although they are by no means free of errors, they are often better than those offered in the specialist dictionaries.

The fundamental problem, as any experienced translator knows, is that – however paradoxical it may sound – even a general dictionary (and *a fortiori* a technical one) is of no use unless the user already knows what is in it. In other words, unless the translator is already broadly familiar with his subject-matter he cannot either choose the best (or in his context the only correct one) of the alternative translations offered by the dictionary or, as the case may be, know whether the one and only translation offered is right. Possible translations can only be evaluated – or thought of in the first place – against a background of knowledge of the SL culture in general and, in the case of technical texts, of the particular subject-matter. The translator must be able to choose *en pleine connaissance de cause.* (The remaining chapters of this book aim to provide the elementary knowledge and comparison of the French and English legal systems which will put a generally competent translator in that position as regards legal translation from French into English as delimited in Section 3.1.) In my experience the only bilingual dictionaries that are of any real use are accordingly the few which either provide plenty of examples of their headwords in use in actual collocations or else are explanatory, i.e. give miniature encyclopaedia-type articles on each headword, explaining its use and its place in the legal system in question. From this point of view, monolingual law dictionaries or encyclopaedias are often more useful than bilingual dictionaries, precisely because they give the definitions and explanations lacking in bilingual dictionaries, which mostly presuppose that the translator has the relevant knowledge.

As regards French–English translation, the only interlingual legal dictionary which combines the merits of offering translations with the advantages of a monolingual dictionary/encyclopaedia is O'Rooney's *Notes on the Criminal Laws and related matters in certain countries* – a United Nations glossary of legal terms together with 'Cursory notes on some systems of law, judicatures and courts', which was apparently never published commercially and has long been out of print. Being multilingual, it provides much information about legal systems that are of little interest to the translator from French, who would have been glad to have more information about the French system, which is nevertheless quite well covered. The author gives most helpful definitions and explanations of terms, and in appropriate cases does not shrink from either offering new translations of his own invention or, on the contrary, indicating that no suggested translation is a sufficiently close equivalent to be acceptable and that the term in question must accordingly be left in the original language. While still invaluable, especially for complete beginners, this splendid work is unfortunately now very much out of date, and there is a great need for an up-to-date bilingual dictionary on the same lines.

By the time the present book is in print, however, the most helpful and comprehensive of French–English legal dictionaries, edited by Frank Bridge, should have been published in a revised and expanded version by the Council of Europe after several years during which it has been available only as an in-house glossary, primarily for the use of Council of Europe staff translators. While not being discursively explanatory like O'Rooney's glossary, the dictionary has the virtually unique merit of offering really usable yet authentic, accurate translations – usually functional equivalents – derived from many years' professional experience of encountering the terms in numerous contexts; and where there is no real English equivalent or neat semantic translation, the editor gives concise definitions or explanations.

In the absence of any modern encyclopaedic French–English legal dictionary, the most useful works are – as hinted above – the available monolingual dictionaries or encyclopaedias. I have found the best of these to be: Curzon's *Dictionary of Law*, Guillien and Vincent's *Lexique de termes juridiques* and two larger and amazingly comprehensive, thorough works, Cornu's *Vocabulaire juridique* and Walker's monumental *Oxford Companion to Law*. The Curzon and Cornu dictionaries are particularly useful as language dictionaries, giving legal terms (verbs and adjectives as well as nouns) which do not denote actual institutions – e.g. 'defeasible', *reçu* (as a past participle) – as well as those that do; while the *Oxford Companion* is preeminent as an encyclopaedic dictionary and contains useful short surveys of many foreign legal systems as well as much historical and biographical material.

Full details of these and other dictionaries which have been consulted in the preparation of this guide are given in the bibliography. In conclusion, it is to be hoped that the optimism displayed by Thomas Reynolds in a 1986 article on current interlingual legal dictionaries proves justified:

> That there are so few really good bilingual dictionaries aimed at the English speaking audience simply reflects the demands of the marketplace and patterns and traditions of use. Americans and other English speaking legal scholars and practitioners have long been reluctant to involve themselves in matters requiring access to foreign materials, legislation and jurisprudence, on a major scale. The situation is now changing and we can expect to see many more scholarly and comprehensive treatments in the near future.[6]

6. T. Reynolds, 'Comparative Legal Dictionaries', *American Journal of Comparative Law*, 34 (1986), 551–8 (p. 558).

PART II

The French legal system: putting translation principles into practice

–4–

French law and English law and their branches

4.1 The concept of law

In keeping with what was said in the Introduction, no attempt will be made here to sketch the historical background to the legal systems of France and England, for which the reader may be referred to the excellent works by René David and by J. H. Merryman listed in the bibliography. Although a knowledge of this background is both fascinating to acquire and useful to possess, it is not essential for the purposes of translation, and the translator here and now must begin with the fact that the two systems are different and accordingly master in some detail the nature of the differences as they currently exist, so as to be able to determine what equivalent English terms are available and precisely how closely they correspond. The main part of this book is designed to assist in that task. In this opening chapter, the aim is to stand well back and try to gain a *vue d'ensemble*, a general picture, of French and English law.

It will be observed that the word 'system' has been used so far. This is deliberate, for the first requirement is that the translator should have a sound grasp of the two systems as wholes. As was shown briefly in Section 1.3, even the written language of the law is used in a wide variety of different contexts – legislation, judgments, legal treatises, pleadings and so on – but none of these can be properly understood other than within the framework of the relevant system as a whole.

The first thing to strike one is that the very conception of law as an area of study and of activity is itself different in France and in England. The Continental conception of law is in general broader than the English one, and in France it encompasses matters dealt with in England under the heads of government, public administration or political science:

A Frenchman [. . .] does not regard the law as something of interest

> only to lawyers. The law is not a restricted domain. It is not the business of judges and practitioners alone, because the law is not limited to litigation. The law is seen as a method of social organisation, always changing, and is thus of primary interest to statesmen and in fact to all citizens.[1]

As a result of this, 'it is an axiom in France that legal studies open all doors. [. . .] The Frenchman considers [. . .] familiarity with the law an almost essential element of a person's general education; the French public does not regard the law as something esoteric and mysterious, as the English regard their common law.'[2] More specifically, for an English lawyer the very idea of law is closely linked to the possibility of bringing an action in the courts, whereas to the French mind the law comprises *all* the rules devised to establish the structures of society and to regulate people's conduct, and these include many which cannot give rise to an action in the courts but are none the less basic to the organisation of the State.

The English word 'law' corresponds to a whole range of words in French, depending on the sense in which it is used. For example, 'a law' (or statute) is *une loi* (a countable noun) and '(the) law' as in the collocation 'in the name of the law' is generally *la loi* (uncountable) or, in some contexts, *la justice* ('to fall foul of the law').[3] '(The) law' as an academic discipline, however, is *le droit*, and this is also the word used for the legal systems and/or law of different countries (*le droit anglais*, etc.) and for the various branches of the law (*le droit pénal*, etc.), which will now be looked at.

4.2 Classifications of law

In most legal systems the law is arranged systematically into categories or branches, though not always for the same purpose in each system. Thus, whereas the distinction between *droit privé* ('private law'[4]) and *droit public* ('public law') is primary and of fundamental practical significance in France (where, as will be

1. R. David, *French Law. Its Structure, Sources, and Methodology*, M. Kindred, trans. (Louisiana State University Press, 1972), p. viii.
2. Ibid., p. 51.
3. For further comments on the use of the word *loi* in the meaning of 'statute' see p. 60 below.
4. Translations which either inherently or in the light of previous discussion present no particular problem and are uncontroversial will be given in brackets after the French without further comment. Obviously in this book – as in a bilingual dictionary – it is primarily the translation of isolated lexical items ('lexemes') that is being dealt with, and in different syntactic contexts these may be realised as different

explained in greater detail in Chapter 6, these different branches are broadly assigned to two different hierarchies of courts), the distinction between private and public law in England has traditionally been made chiefly in order to facilitate academic exposition of the law, although it is now of growing practical importance for procedural purposes[5] given the spectacular increase in the use and scope of the public-law remedy of judicial review of administrative action;[6] none the less, public-law disputes are still governed by the same fundamental rules of common law that apply to private-law disputes. By contrast, practical importance attaches to the distinction between *droit civil* ('civil law') and *droit pénal* ('criminal law') both in France and in England (where it is the major division of the law).

The distinction made between private and public law – which dates from Roman times – rests on the principle that the same rules cannot apply both to the State and to private citizens (because, for example, the State can hardly be expected to enforce judicial decisions which affect its interests adversely with as much willingness as it does those which affect only private interests: even in English law, public funds cannot be attached to enforce a court decision). Accordingly, public law governs relations to which the State (or a subdivision of it, such as a *département*, or a State-owned enterprise or a public authority) is a party, while private law governs the rights and duties of private persons and corporations.[7]

It must be borne in mind that such divisions of the law – and the subdivisions to be indicated shortly – are not watertight, although they are widely accepted. A book entitled *Droit du travail* ('labour

---

grammatical items. Thus, while it might be suggested that *détention provisoire* should be translated as 'detention pending trial', a translator adopting this suggestion would probably want to translate the collocation *décisions de mise en détention provisoire* as 'decisions *to detain* (accused persons) pending trial' as being more in keeping with natural English style than, say, 'decisions on (the) detention (of accused persons) pending trial'. (Excessive use of nouns and prepositions instead of verbs and adjectives or possessives in an English translation is a classic symptom of poor translation from French, e.g. 'After the ratification of the treaty by the Government of France' instead of 'After the French Government's ratification of the treaty' or, better still, 'After the French Government had ratified the treaty'.)

5. In two leading cases in 1982 the House of Lords laid down that in cases where only public-law rights were involved, would-be litigants had to pursue their claims for relief against administrative bodies by means of an application for judicial review. In so doing it effectively established a private law/public law dichotomy for the first time in England.

6. In 1974 there were 160 applications for judicial review; in 1985, 1,230.

7. Note that social institutions like marriage and divorce – in which the State has an interest – remain legal relations between private persons alone, not between private persons and the State; and they are consequently governed by private law. Public law is one thing, rules imposed for reasons of public policy are another.

law' or 'industrial law'), for instance, will automatically deal with questions both of private law and of public law (e.g. the duty of employers to pay social-security contributions). And, of course, some classifications resulting from a more or less arbitrary grouping of rules in one legal system may have no counterpart in another (e.g. the concepts of the law of tort in English law and the *droit des obligations* in French law). Furthermore, as elements of public law creep into every sector of human activity with the growing intervention of the State in the lives of its citizens, new, hybrid, catch-all branches of law are formed from the amalgamation of all the relevant areas of private and public law – *droit économique* ('economic law'), *droit de l'environnement* ('environment(al) law') and *droit rural* ('rural law') are all examples of such *droit mixte* ('hybrid law') – and the validity of even the supposedly fundamental distinction between private and public law seems, at any rate to an outside observer, to be put in question.

4.3 Private law

Private law proper consists principally of *droit civil* ('civil law'), the most venerable and highly sophisticated branch of French law, based largely on the famous Napoleonic *Code civil* ('Civil Code') of 1804 (as since amended). It should be noted here that the polysemous term 'civil law' – seven or eight definitions of it are given in Walker's *Oxford Companion to Law* – means in this context *ius civile*, the law applicable to ordinary citizens in ordinary relations with one another (as distinct from commercial law, administrative law and criminal law or from military or ecclesiastical law) and not '(a system of) law based on Roman law' – the sense in which it has mostly been used in this book so far, i.e. (the) civil law in contrast to (the) common law.

French civil law is in turn subdivided, in the Code and in textbooks, into: *droit des personnes* ('law of persons'), including the legal capacity of minors and persons of unsound mind, domicile, naming and other personal attributes – there is no equivalent separate branch of English law; *droit de la famille* ('family law'), including marriage and divorce and the relationships between parents and children, as in English law; *les régimes matrimoniaux* ('matrimonial property regimes'[8]), i.e. the *régime contractuel* ('contractual regime'),

8. 'Regime' is preferable to the commoner translation 'system' here, because there are several regimes making up an overall system.

Diagram 4.1 The main branches of private law

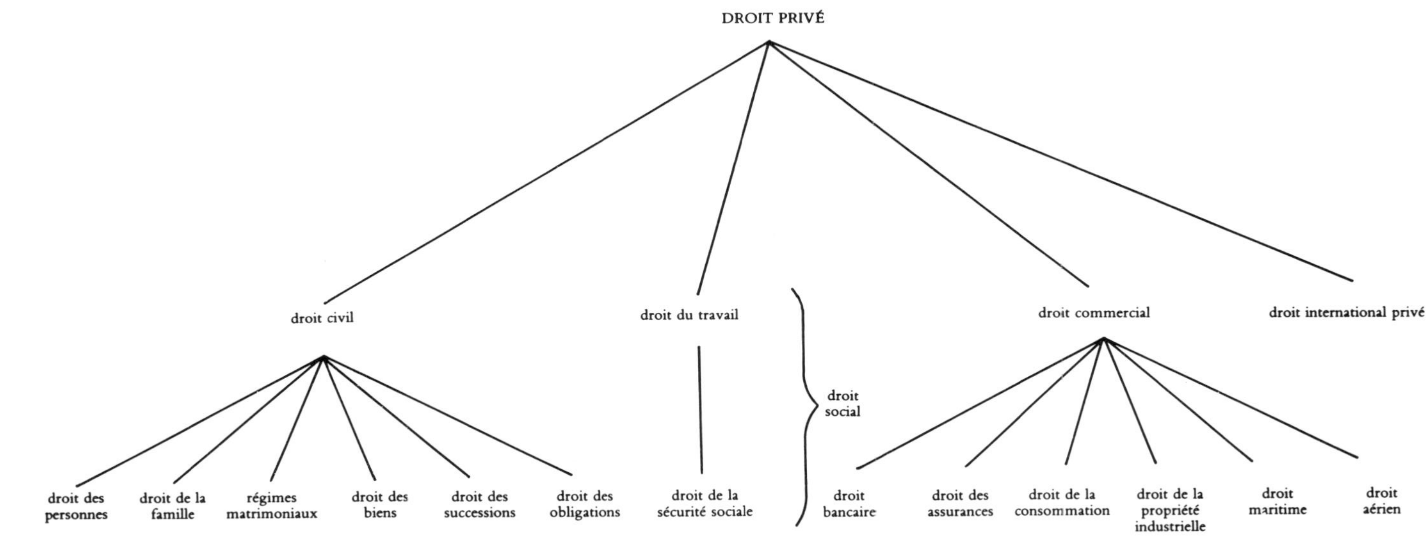

covering *contrats de mariage* ('marriage contracts'[9] or 'marriage settlements'[10]), and the alternative *régime légal* (the 'statutory regime' of *communauté de biens* – 'community (of) property') (again, not recognised as a distinct branch of law in England)[11]; *droit des biens* ('law of property', 'property law'), covering not only real property and personal property as in English law but also matters such as conversion (in England part of the law of tort) and other matters which in England are dealt with in the law of trusts or in procedure; *droit des successions* ('law of succession'), covering wills and intestacies, as in England, but under which head *libéralités* ('gifts') are also studied; and, finally, *droit des obligations*: this subdivision, which is not a distinct branch in English law, covers not only the law of contract but also obligations arising under what in England would be the law of tort, and the rules about unjust enrichment which are considered in England under the heads of quasi-contract and restitution – and alongside contract it also includes *sûretés* ('suretyship'); the term *droit des obligations* accordingly cannot be translated as 'law of contract' as both Harrap's and Herbst and Readett's dictionaries suggest – a wider term must be found, and the best would seem to be the word-for-word rendering 'law of obligations',[12] provided it is borne in mind that it is not the obligations of common law which are meant (which correspond roughly to debts).

It is convenient to mention at this point that *procédure civile* ('civil procedure', by some French writers termed also *droit judiciaire privé*), which, like the substantive civil law itself, is codified (in the *Nouveau Code de procédure civile* – 'New Code of Civil Procedure' – of 1975), is sometimes classified alongside *droit civil* as private law, as one might expect, but sometimes as public law, as being concerned with the public administration of justice.

A recognisably distinct new area of private law has grown from civil law: *droit du travail* ('labour law' or 'industrial law'), based on the *Code du travail* of 1973 and later legislation, and administered by separate courts at first instance. Another distinctive feature is that

9. A word-for-word translation in terms of English law, but both a word-for-word translation and a functional equivalent in terms of the Scottish system.

10. A functional equivalent in terms of English law.

11. It is to be noted, however, that the statutory minimum rules governing the financial aspects of marriage (the *régime matrimonial primaire* introduced by an Act of 1965 and which could perhaps best be translated as the 'basic matrimonial property regime'), which the parties to a marriage cannot contract out of, are dealt with as part of family law.

12. Doucet offers 'law of obligations' under *droit (des obligations)* but, misleadingly and inconsistently, 'civil responsibility' under *obligations (droit des)*.

labour law not surprisingly incorporates many principles of public law, and indeed the subdivision of *droit de la sécurité sociale* ('social-security law') – an offshoot of labour law which in its turn has become largely distinct from its parent branch – is now often classified as an autonomous branch of law separate both from private and from public law, though it remains within the jurisdiction of the private-law courts. The term *droit social* ('welfare law') is sometimes encountered as a general term embracing both labour law and social-security law (regarded in that case as two separate branches of law).

What of the rest of private law, lying outside the scope of civil law as embodied in the Civil Code? Two main areas need to be mentioned.

Firstly, *droit commercial*. The apparent identity between the French term and the English 'commercial law' is misleading, and a careful distinction must be made between the two concepts, which are very different. Commercial law in France is a body of law distinct from civil law and contained in the Napoleonic *Code de commerce* ('Commercial Code') of 1807 as amended, and again is administered by separate, commercial courts at first instance. It is the law governing, *inter alia*, companies and partnerships, trademarks, patents, negotiable instruments and also bankruptcy (which in France is available *only* to businessmen). Commercial law in England, on the other hand, is not a separate branch of law, and the term signifies merely those topics – taught under that head but drawn mostly from the law of property and of contract – relevant to business and commercial practice (the law being the same whether the transactions concerned are commercial or between friends: there is no distinct legal category of trader or of acts of trade).

In English law there is no separate body of rules governing commercial as opposed to private transactions. 'Commercial law', it is true, has also a separate procedural meaning, in which it may be said to comprise commercial litigation, i.e. the causes of action which may be entered in the 'commercial list' in the charge of one of the judges of the Queen's Bench Division of the High Court, sitting in what since 1970 has been known as the Commercial Court, where special, simplified rules of procedure apply; but the judge who takes the commercial list applies the same legal principles and rules of substantive law that he would if he were exercising his judicial function outside the Commercial Court. Historically, just as in the seventeenth and eighteenth centuries the medieval 'law merchant' – mercantile law and customs – was in

England absorbed into the common law, the law of the land and its citizens at large, so in the sixteenth and seventeenth centuries the 'courts merchant' had been absorbed into the common-law courts.

In France too the historical reasons for the distinction between *droit civil* and *droit commercial* have long since ceased to apply and, except perhaps in the sub-branch of *droit maritime* ('maritime/admiralty law'), the distinction has indeed much diminished, the main subsisting differences being procedural. In some other civil-law countries with more recent codifications, such as Switzerland and Italy, the distinction has in fact been abandoned altogether.

The main subdivisions of *droit commercial* other than maritime law are *droit bancaire* ('law of banking', 'banking law'), *droit des assurances* ('insurance law'), *droit de la consommation* ('consumer law' or 'consumer-protection law'), *droit de la propriété industrielle* ('industrial-property law') and *droit aérien* ('air law'); all contain substantial elements of public law.

Despite the differences between *droit commercial* and 'commercial law', it is clear that the latter must be used to translate the former – in accordance with the 'breakfast principle' alluded to on p. 21 above: the two concepts are not *utterly* different, and there is no possibility that 'commercial law' could be taken, when applied to the French system, as referring to anything other than *droit commercial*.

It is perhaps worth adding here that from *droit commercial* has grown what academic writers term *droit économique*, the hybrid body of private-law and public-law rules governing the organisation and development of the industrial economy, whether private, public or a mixture of the two. This term is better translated word for word as 'economic law' than as 'business law', which is largely synonymous in English with 'commercial law' and is accordingly best kept for translating *droit des affaires*, a term often used as a synonym of *droit commercial* but strictly denoting a larger concept, again above the distinction between private and public law, covering all the aspects of business and economic activity as a whole.

The other remaining division of private law is *droit international privé* ('private international law'). This includes *conflit(s) de lois* ('conflict of laws' or 'choice of laws'), *conflit(s) de juridictions* ('conflict of jurisdiction'), *exécution des jugements étrangers* ('enforcement of foreign judgments'), *nationalité* ('nationality') and *condition des étrangers* ('status of aliens'). As its name would suggest, it is usually classed as part of private law,[13] but it *can* be regarded as dealing

13. It has nothing to do with (public) international law, and for this reason is

primarily with matters of national sovereignty, which is a public-law concept.

4.4 Criminal law

Before the content of public law is examined, it is appropriate to mention at this point a branch of law which lies uneasily between – or astride – private and public law: *droit pénal* ('criminal law'). Criminal justice in France is administered by the same judges as administer civil (i.e. private) law, though in courts which are technically distinct (but in practice only the *cour d'assises* ('Assize Court') has exclusively criminal jurisdiction). Traditionally it has been the domain of *privatistes* ('specialists in private law') and treated as part of private law. In content, however, criminal law and procedure are increasingly often classified, more logically, with public law. Such a classification reflects the view – more consistent with reality – that crime is primarily a matter of concern to society at large and that it is thus the State's responsibility to prevent and punish it, whereas formerly criminal law was held to regulate private-law relations between a person who caused damage and the person injured (or his family). Although criminal law has thus now virtually become a branch of public law, public-law specialists still deal with it in only one exceptional case, namely if crimes are committed by the President of the Republic or members of the government in their official capacity. For most practical purposes, however, criminal law is treated as an autonomous discipline.

4.5 Public law

The main, if somewhat artificial, subdivision within public law is into *droit constitutionnel* ('constitutional law') and *droit administratif* ('administrative law'). Although this distinction is largely one of convenience, corresponding broadly to the one between legislative and executive power, it is perhaps not wholly true to say, as do Kahn-Freund, Lévy and Rudden,[14] that its sole *raison d'être* in both

---

sometimes referred to in English as 'international private law', a term which still, however, misleadingly conceals the fact that it is part of each country's *national* private law which deals with private-law relations having an international aspect or element.

14. Sir Otto Kahn-Freund, C. Lévy and B. Rudden, *A Source-book on French Law*, 2nd edn (Clarendon Press, 1979), p. 203.

Diagram 4.2 The main branches of public law

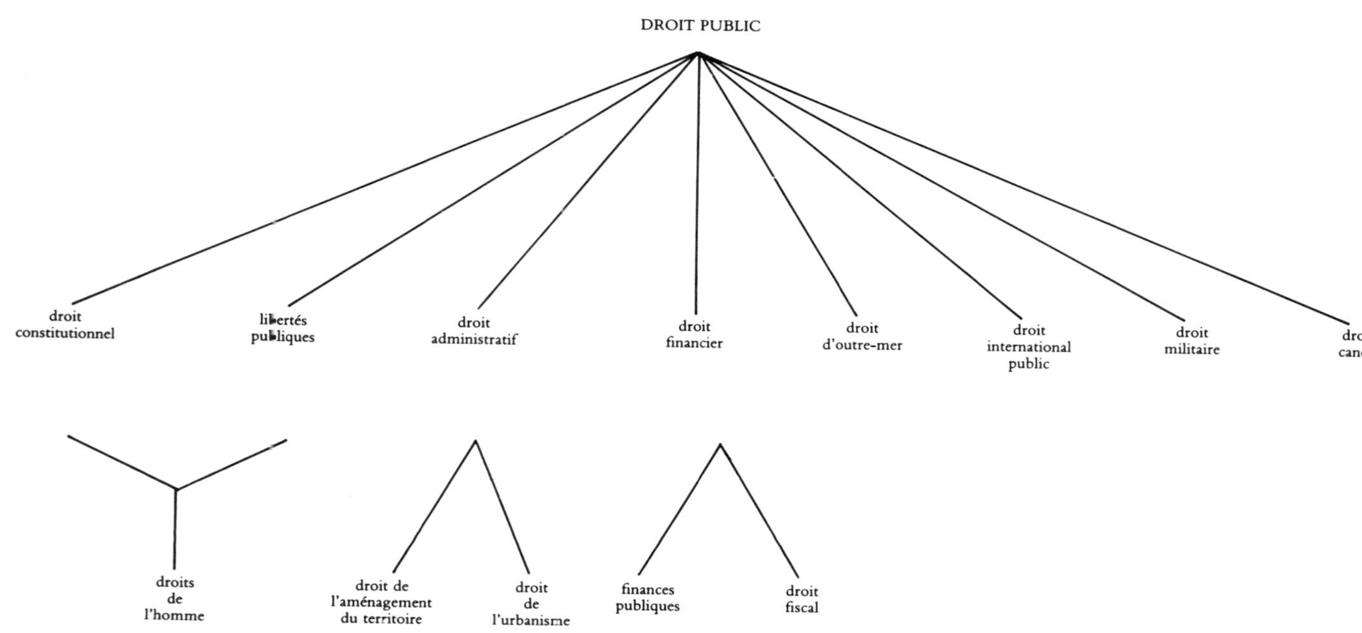

English and French law is to facilitate exposition, since in France unlike England strictly constitutional questions and administrative questions are determined by separate courts.

Neither *droit constitutionnel* nor *droit administratif* corresponds in content to English constitutional law or administrative law. France has a written constitution; England does not. For a French lawyer, constitutional law in its narrower sense is simply the body of rules contained in the Constitution (currently the 1958 one), whereas in England it is left to the lawyers to decide what is proper to be included in the domain of constitutional law. English constitutional law gives an important place to the protection of civil liberties – yet these lie outside the scope of *droit constitutionnel* and are covered, in France, in books on *libertés publiques* ('civil liberties') as a separate branch of public law, although there is no longer any rational ground for this distinction; a sub-branch of *droit constitutionnel* and *libertés publiques* taken together is *droits de l'homme* ('human rights'), which are also protected under (public) international law.

French books on constitutional law cover political science as a whole, setting forth the various modern political systems, with the French constitutional system being considered as one among others (rather as in Montesquieu's *De l'Esprit des lois*) – and even then the structure of the supranational French Community is outlined and dealt with separately in books on *droit d'outre-mer* ('overseas law'), formerly *droit colonial* ('colonial law'). This reflects the wider conception of *droit constitutionnel* as 'the subject in which historical perspective is combined with the public opinion of the times in the process of distilling the principles of general public law recognised and enforced by the courts'.[15] In France the provisions of constitutional law are indeed regarded not only as pure public law – concerned primarily with the State and its organisation and only minimally relevant to the individual – but accordingly as political rather than legal;[16] and, as will be seen in Section 6.9, the body which determines constitutional questions has more the appearance of a political council than of a court and at present has no jurisdiction to adjudicate on individuals' constitutional rights (or even to entertain applications from private citizens at all).

Much of what has just been said about the differences between *droit constitutionnel* and constitutional law applies to the differences

15. R. David and H. P. de Vries, *The French Legal System* (Oceana Publications, 1958), p. 63.

16. Cf. the Spanish term for constitutional law, *derecho político*.

between *droit administratif* and administrative law. Like *droit constitutionnel, droit administratif* tends to merge with political science, and part of it is little more than a description of French administrative practice – the appointment of civil servants and the distribution of their functions. To that must be added the substantive rules governing public officials' and agencies' relations with the public and with private corporations; and the remedies available for breaches of these rules, together with procedure in the administrative courts. Two other major topics worth mentioning separately are *droit de l'aménagement du territoire* and *droit de l'urbanisme*. These would probably be jointly covered by the single English term 'planning law', the former relating to regional planning, the latter to town planning.

There is no written source of administrative law in France comparable either to the Constitution or to the Civil Code, and much administrative law consists of case-law built up by the courts, although a consolidation of the various statutes applied by the administrative courts exists in the form published as the *Code administratif* ('Administrative Code') – but this is not a true code in the sense of a systematic arrangement of basic principles on the lines of the *Code civil*. Indeed, exceptionally in French law, it can be said, in the words of the old English adage, that remedies have preceded rights.

In England, by contrast, it was virtually true until quite recently[17] that there was no such thing as administrative law, public bodies being subject to essentially the same rules as any private citizen. The special provisions which apply to the Crown and its agents in English law are distinctions made *within* the common law and do not derive from a separate body of law – there is no suggestion that the common law as a whole should not apply to State agencies; whereas the existence of administrative law as a wholly separate branch of law in France springs from the basic distinction made between private and public law. In so far as it can now be said to exist, administrative law in England is still some-

17. As late as 1963 Lord Reid was able to say: 'We [in England] do not have a developed system of administrative law – perhaps because until fairly recently we did not need it' (*Ridge* v. *Baldwin* [1963] 2 All ER 66 at 76). But by 1971 Lord Denning was noting: 'It may truly now be said that we have developed a system of administrative law' (*Breen* v. *Amalgamated Engineering Union* [1971] 1 All ER 1148 at 1153). And in 1986 Sir Harry (Lord Justice) Woolf commented: 'I find it difficult to believe that there has been any other period of our legal history where a sphere of law has developed in such a rapid and exciting manner as administrative law over the period since I started practice'; in 'Public Law – Private Law: Why the Divide?', *Public Law* (1986) 220–38 (p. 220).

thing quite different in kind from *droit administratif*. English lawyers having become aware that certain problems do arise only in respect of public bodies, they have given some consideration, under the head of administrative law, to such problems as how administrative regulations and orders should be prepared and on what grounds they may be criticised or quashed, how government departments should proceed before taking decisions in individual cases, and what remedies are available against such decisions; in other words, some of the topics covered by *droit administratif* but not all of them and, most importantly, not as a separate body of law – indeed, a major characteristic of English administrative law has been the totally unplanned and piecemeal development of administrative bodies and their very diverse powers. And where, for example, a public body or one of its officials does unlawful damage to an individual's property, it will, in England, be subject to the same private-law rules and remedies as any private citizen.

For all these important differences between, on the one hand, *droit constitutionnel* and *droit administratif* and, on the other, 'constitutional law' and 'administrative law', there is again, as with *droit commercial* earlier, not sufficient reason to reject the formally equivalent translations 'constitutional law' and 'administrative law' respectively; indeed, any other translation is simply unthinkable, as there are no functionally equivalent alternatives.

The other main branches of public law are *droit financier* ('financial law'), which covers *finances publiques* ('public finance(s)') and *droit fiscal* ('tax law'); *droit international public* or *droit des gens* ('public international law' or 'the law of nations'); *droit militaire* ('military law'); and *droit canon/canonique* ('canon law'), occasionally referred to as *droit ecclésiastique* ('ecclesiastical law').

4.6 *Droit commun*

This chapter should not be concluded without some explanation of a term frequently met with and likely to baffle or mislead any native English speaker approaching French law for the first time: *droit commun*. From what has been said so far, and notwithstanding that the Harrap and the Herbst and Readett dictionaries give 'common law' as a translation, it should be evident that *droit commun* has nothing to do with the English common law – although the idea of a common law is by no means irrelevant. *Droit commun* is not actually a branch of law at all, and understanding the concept is not made any easier by the fact that the term has two slightly different meanings in this context (the meaning *un droit commun*, 'a joint right', is being disregarded here) – although, as it happens, a single translation will usually cover either meaning. The narrower meaning is 'the law of the Codes', and more particularly of the Civil Code, as contrasted with *droit spécial* ('special law') or any *loi d'exception* ('special statute'[18]), i.e. legislation overriding the general provisions of the Codes. The broader meaning is 'the law or rules ordinarily applying in any given branch of law', and a good illustration of its use in this sense is given in Bridge's dictionary: 'de droit commun celui qui veut obtenir l'annulation d'un acte [. . .]', 'the general rule is that someone seeking to have a transaction set aside [. . .]'. Both meanings of *droit commun* can be conveniently covered by the term 'ordinary law', although, as shown in Bridge's example, the term 'general rule' may prove more appropriate, and one may wish in other cases to qualify the term 'ordinary law', e.g. *prisonnier de droit commun*, 'a prisoner convicted under the ordinary criminal law' (as opposed, say, to prisoners sentenced for political offences or by special courts).

In this connection it may be helpful to point out too that while the term *exorbitant* can mean 'unconscionable' or 'unreasonable', e.g. when applied to penalty clauses in contracts, it is also frequently used elliptically to mean *exorbitant du droit commun*, notably in the expression *clauses exorbitantes du droit commun*, 'terms [commonly found in government contracts] to which the ordinary law [i.e. civil law as opposed to administrative law] does not apply'.[19]

18. Only occasionally will the French term refer to an 'emergency law'.
19. For a similar distinction between different classes of courts – *juridictions de droit commun* and *juridictions d'exception* – see Section 6.2.

–5–

Legislation

5.1 Legislation as a source of law

The bulk of the substantive law in the branches described in the previous chapter is to be found in legislation, which has been the primary source of law in France since the Revolution – as it has only comparatively recently become in England, where until this century case-law remained predominant. Judicial decisions in criminal[1] and (non-administrative) civil cases nearly always purport to rest on a legislative provision. Much of this legislation is, as we have just seen, codified but by no means all of it: it is worth reiterating that administrative law has never been codified, as opposed to merely consolidated, and pointing out that some of the post-Napoleonic codes are similarly no more than consolidations of pre-existing statutes or else collections of unconsolidated ones rather than being in any sense a 'fresh start' like the original Civil Code. None the less, the corpus of modern French private and criminal law is composed of the five Napoleonic codes as amended by subsequent legislation (or replaced), and although there remain many separate statutes, it is apparent from the expression *loi d'exception* referred to at the end of the last chapter that these are still regarded as exceptions to the norm of a code, and they are wont to be construed very strictly by the courts. And as the true codes are regarded as expressions of natural law and equity, their principles, though not binding on the administrative courts, are not rejected in administrative law without good reason. Constitutional law, of course, is based on the Constitution.

The intention in this chapter is not to describe the legislative process as such but to explain the various types of law that result from it.

1. Cf. the adage *nullum crimen, nulla poena sine lege*: only a statute can define a crime and prescribe a penalty.

5.2 *Lois* versus *règlements* and *ordonnances*

Although the word *législation* exists (e.g. *la législation française, législation financière*), the commoner French word corresponding to 'legislation' in English is *la loi* or *les lois*. Thus Article 34 of the Constitution states: 'La loi est votée par le Parlement'. In the narrow sense, *lois* are statutes; but the word has a larger sense in which it includes the Constitution, treaties and administrative regulations, all of which are substantively of a legislative nature (*lois au sens matériel*) – general measures issued by duly constituted authority – in contrast to *lois au sens formel*, a term applicable only to Acts of Parliament.

This distinction arises because in France the power to make rules is not vested exclusively in Parliament but, by Articles 34 and 37 of the Constitution, is divided between the legislature (Parliament) and the executive (the government, i.e. the Prime Minister and his ministers, none of whom may also sit as an elected member of Parliament). These two different types of rule have different names: Parliament may enact *lois* ('statutes') in the areas listed in Article 34 of the Constitution, including notably such matters as serious criminal offences and the basic principles of the law of property, contract and tort; while under Article 37 it is for the government to legislate by means of *règlements* ('regulations') in all other spheres. And under Article 38 of the Constitution, the government may ask Parliament for leave during a limited period to legislate even in the domain normally reserved for parliamentary legislation; and if so authorised (by means of a blanket *loi d'habilitation*, 'enabling Act'), it will proceed by way of *ordonnances* ('ordinances').[2] These have the force of a regulation until the government has laid before Parliament a ratification bill, when they acquire the force of law. If the bill is not laid within the period specified in the enabling Act or

2. Although P. Thody and H. Evans in their *Faux Amis & Key Words* (Athlone Press, 1985) claim that this term is much wider than 'ordinance' in English, they do not produce any evidence to support that statement and their proposed rendering 'decree' is needed as the translation of *décret*. 'Ordinance' is admittedly hardly used, if at all, as a term of art in modern English law, but its ordinary meaning is wholly appropriate to the present context. An alternative translation here – and the only appropriate one in judicial contexts – is 'Order', a standard English term for a statutory instrument, i.e. subordinate or delegated legislation (which in a limited sense is what *ordonnances* are, unlike the *règlements* that the government is entitled to make under the power conferred on it by Article 37, i.e. without being specially empowered by statute to do so); but 'order' is also a standard translation of *arrêté* (see Section 5.4). Under the Third and Fourth Republics, such instruments were called *décrets-lois* ('legislative decrees').

if Parliament rejects the bill, the ordinances lose all force.

Whereas statutes, once promulgated, cannot be subjected to any form of review as to their constitutionality[3] and must accordingly be applied even if incompatible with one or more principles in the Constitution, regulations (including *ordonnances* until ratified) must always conform with the Constitution, with statute law and with what are known in French administrative law as the *principes généraux du droit* ('general principles of law'), and can accordingly be challenged in the administrative courts.

5.3 *Lois*

There are several different special kinds of statute apart from *lois ordinaires* ('ordinary Acts'), and they require special legislative procedures; but all statutes start out as either *projets de loi* or *propositions de loi*. These two kinds of 'bill' (which is usually an adequate translation for both terms) correspond roughly to 'government bills' – in France tabled by the Prime Minister – and 'private members' bills' (which can be used as translations in contexts where the distinction is important). All statutes likewise have to be promulgated in a *décret de promulgation* ('promulgation decree') signed by the President as Head of State. Promulgation is somewhat akin to the giving of the Royal Assent to legislation in Britain but is less of a mere formality, as by Article 10 of the Constitution the President may require Parliament to reconsider any bill submitted to him – and in practice, of course, he can influence legislation merely by indicating that he has reservations about a given bill during its passage through Parliament and thus that he would be minded to refer it back to Parliament if it were submitted to him unaltered for him to promulgate. The official date of an Act will be the date of promulgation (which must take place within a fortnight of the bill's being sent to the government by Parliament), but the enactment cannot take effect until it has been published.

There are three main types of special Act. Firstly, *lois constitutionnelles* ('constitutional Acts/laws'): as their name suggests, these are statutes which amend the Constitution. (And it may be noted in passing that *(la) loi constitutionnelle* is also used to refer to the Constitution itself.)

3. As regards the subordination of statutes to treaties, however, see note 34 on p. 87 below.

Secondly, however, there are also Acts which do not alter the Constitution but have a status approaching that of constitutional legislation, viz. *lois organiques*. The purpose of these basic laws, which are referred to no fewer than nineteen times in the Constitution, is to, as it were, fill out the Constitution by enacting detailed provisions implementing the general principles of the Constitution, and in particular to provide for the establishment and operation of public authorities. The term *loi organique* is often translated as 'organic law', but the expression is neither a natural English one – there are few attestations of it in *The Oxford English Dictionary* – nor one familiar to common lawyers, and its meaning is not obvious. Perhaps a more transparently meaningful and English-sounding rendering would be the semantic equivalent 'institutional Act' – one of the possibilities suggested by Bridge.

Thirdly and lastly, there are laws passed by means of a referendum – *lois référendaires*. Since 'referendum Acts/laws' is perhaps unduly elliptical, this term is probably better rendered by the definition just given. Only major legislation – such as constitutional laws and bills relating to the organisation of public authorities, to Community agreements or to international treaties which would have effects on France's institutions – is liable to this treatment; and if the bill concerned is approved, the President promulgates it in the usual way.

In addition to these three special types of Act there are three other terms descriptive of legislation which are commonly met with and should accordingly be mentioned here. The first of these (which is in fact midway between a mere description of legislation and an actual category like *loi organique*, since it usually appears as part of the Act's title) is *loi d'orientation*. The term denotes an Act which lays down in advance a general policy to be implemented over a period of time; it is not easy to translate. On its own, one might call it a 'general Act' in English or perhaps a 'policy Act' or even combine both these as 'general policy Act'. In the title of a statute there might be other possibilities. One could proceed as if the qualification *d'orientation* were not there, e.g. *loi d'orientation de l'enseignement supérieur* could be translated simply as 'Higher Education Act'; or one could qualify in some way: 'Higher Education (General Principles/Policy) Act' – perhaps less convincing as the title of an Act in English; and, finally, in some areas of legislation the word *orientation* might be translated as 'development', e.g. Doucet's rendering of *loi d'orientation agricole* as 'Agricultural Development Act'.

The other two terms to be mentioned go together as a pair: *loi impérative* and *loi supplétive*. A *loi impérative* is a rule[4] (of private law) that is mandatory – i.e. overrides any contrary wishes of the parties (e.g. to a contract) or, as it is often put in English law, applies 'any agreement to the contrary notwithstanding' – as a matter of *ordre public* ('public policy'[5]); indeed, *loi d'ordre public* is a synonymous though somewhat broader term, and it is the Civil Code which, in Article 6, provides that laws relating to public policy or morality cannot be derogated from by private agreements. Thus, for example, an incurably ill person cannot by an exercise of his own will lawfully overcome the prohibition on murder by requesting euthanasia; or again, courts will in certain circumstances refuse to uphold unfair contract terms.

The opposite of a *loi impérative* is a *loi supplétive*, a rule that either applies in the absence of any expressed intention to the contrary or else is designed to supplement an inadequately expressed agreement; in the latter case it may be simply an aid to construction or it may be the expression of a policy that the legislature considers generally desirable rather than of merely the presumed intent of the parties. Examples here would be the rules on intestacy; and the terms that an English court will read into a contract if necessary, in order to give it business efficacy.

Some French statutes expressly state that they are mandatory, while others state in terms that they yield to the contrary intention of the parties. Many, however, are silent on the subject, and it is then for the courts and legal scholars (whose importance will be discussed in Chapter 7) to determine the matter – one of many instances in which the French courts, while in theory having a purely interpretative rôle, in practice have considerable law-making power.

In view of the foregoing, it would seem that the best translations of the pair of terms are 'mandatory rule/law' and 'non-mandatory rule/law', the renderings used by Kahn-Freund, Lévy and Rudden. For *loi supplétive* another possibility might be 'directory rule', the adjective 'directory' occasionally being used by the English judiciary with reference to procedural rules, in contrast with 'mandatory'.

4. Despite the use of the word *loi*, the French expression is applied also to non-statutory rules, as is its antonym *loi supplétive*.

5. The French term in other contexts can also mean 'public order', of course; and even in the present context it arguably does not correspond exactly to 'public policy' in the sense in which it is normally used by English lawyers, though no other translation seems possible. See further Sir Otto Kahn-Freund, C. Lévy and B. Rudden, *A Source-book on French Law*, 2nd edn (Clarendon Press, 1979), pp. 241–2.

5.4 *Règlements, arrêtés* and *circulaires*

The main types of *loi* having been reviewed, a word must be said about the different kinds of rule that can be enacted by the executive. The generic term *règlement* in fact covers a range of rules and decisions, with various names, that can be made under inherent powers by the whole hierarchy of executive and administrative authorities from the government down to the local mayor.

The most important of these instruments are *décrets* ('decrees'), which are issued by the President or the Prime Minister after the *Conseil d'État* has been consulted (see Sections 6.6 and 6.7). By Article 21 of the Constitution, the power to make the regulations provided for in Article 37 (mentioned in Section 5.2 above) is vested in the Prime Minister, but *décrets en Conseil des ministres* ('decrees in Cabinet'), i.e. adopted after deliberation in Cabinet, are signed by the President, under Article 13 of the Constitution.[6] Decrees fall into two classes as to their content: those enacted under the *pouvoir réglementaire* ('regulation-making/regulatory power') conferred by Article 21 of the Constitution – *décrets autonomes* ('autonomous decrees'), also referred to as *règlements autonomes* ('autonomous regulations'); and those which are enacted at the request of the legislature for the purpose of implementing Acts of Parliament – *décrets d'application* ('implementing decrees'), also referred to as *règlements d'application* ('implementing regulations'). Only the latter are truly subordinate or delegated legislation.

The other types of regulation are fairly rapidly dealt with. Ministers singly and jointly may issue *arrêtés ministériels* ('ministerial orders') and *arrêtés interministériels* ('interministerial orders') respectively. *Arrêtés* may also be issued by prefects – *arrêtés préfectoraux*; by mayors – *arrêtés municipaux*; and by other administrative authorities – e.g. directors of education (*recteurs*), who issue *arrêtés rectoraux*. Here the word *arrêté* has to be translated according to each particular context. In the case of individual officials such as prefects or directors of education, the word will often best be rendered simply as 'prefectoral, etc., decision' (or 'decision of the prefect, etc.') rather than 'order'. In the case of an *arrêté* issued by a town council or other corporate authority (or an official on its behalf), the translation 'by-law' will sometimes be the most appropriate – e.g. 'municipal by-law' for *arrêté municipal*.

6. Procedurally speaking, decrees that are not *décrets en Conseil des ministres* are either *décrets en Conseil d'État* ('decrees in the Conseil d'État') or *décrets simples* ('ordinary decrees').

Finally, mention may be made of administrative *circulaires* ('circulars'), which are usually deemed by the *Conseil d'État* to have the status of regulations if they contain instructions to civil servants.

–6–

The courts

6.1 *Cours, tribunaux* and *juridictions*

Before the organisation of the French courts is discussed, a word is necessary about the various French terms meaning 'court' and the translation of them.

It should be noted at the outset that in English there are two words available: a general term, 'court', and a (usually) narrower term, 'tribunal'. Tribunals are normally bodies exercising administrative or (more commonly) judicial functions, but with limited or special jurisdiction. They often consist of lay assessors with a chairman who is legally qualified but is not necessarily a judge – e.g. industrial tribunals, rent tribunals, disciplinary tribunals – and they are never called 'courts'. The distinction does not correspond to the one between superior courts and inferior courts – the Employment Appeal Tribunal, for instance, counts as a superior court, while magistrates' courts are inferior courts. In their broadest sense, both terms can also be generic: a tribunal (in the narrow sense) is a special kind of court; and a court is a type of tribunal (in the broad sense[1]).

The situation is very different when one comes to French terminology in these matters. Although there is no formal division into superior and inferior courts, the higher courts are mostly called *cours* and all deliver *arrêts*, while the lower ones are mostly called *tribunaux* and all deliver *jugements*. But there is a third, general term, *juridiction* (as a countable noun), which is apparently superordinate (linguistically) to the other two: any *cour* or *tribunal* (or even an individual judge) could be described as a *juridiction*, whereas some *juridictions* are *cours* and others *tribunaux*. How are these terms to be translated, therefore?

One thing is clear: the French *tribunal* does not, in the usual, narrow sense just defined, correspond to the English term 'tribunal'

1. Cf. 'an independent and impartial tribunal' – a requisite of a fair trial under Article 6 of the European Convention on Human Rights (1950).

in *its* usual, narrow sense above. It should be translated simply as 'court' – or 'inferior/lower court' or 'court of first instance' if the hierarchical feature is relevant and important. Similarly, *cour* will also normally be translated as 'court' or possibly 'superior/higher/ appellate court'. *Juridiction* too must be translated as 'court', though in the plural in collocations such as *les juridictions françaises* it might be rendered as 'courts and tribunals', but it would not normally be necessary to say anything more than 'the French courts' in the instance quoted.[2] Occasionally, as when the *chambre d'accusation* (see p. 82 below) and the *juge d'instruction* (see Section 8.4) are referred to together as *juridictions d'instruction*, the term may have to be translated as, say, 'judicial authority'.

In short, the three French terms are in practice generally to be translated by a single English word, because the distinctions between *cour*, *tribunal* and *juridiction*, in so far as they correspond to distinctions in the English judicial system at all, are not reflected in the English language system. Similarly, *arrêt* and *jugement* are both usually translatable simply as 'decision' or 'judgment', as seems linguistically appropriate ('in a decision in 1960 the court held . . .', 'in its judgment the court makes clear . . .').

These general terms having been disposed of, it is time to look in detail at the way in which the French courts are organised.

6.2 Classifications of courts

France has essentially a dual system of courts, consisting of two quite separate *ordres* ('hierarchies' or 'sets'): the *ordre judiciaire* and the *ordre administratif*. The *juridictions de l'ordre judiciaire* are the ordinary (civil and criminal) courts, which have jurisdiction unless a case involves the State or a State employee or corporation as a

2. It should be noted, however, that just as 'tribunal' in English is occasionally used in the wider sense of a person or persons having power to determine claims or settle disputes, so in French *tribunal* is sometimes used as a generic term more or less synonymous with *juridiction* (in which usage a *cour would* be a *tribunal*, contrary to what was said above). The French term corresponding to 'tribunal' in the article of the Human Rights Convention mentioned in note 1 above is indeed *tribunal*. Cf. also M. Waline, quoted on p. 208 of Sir Otto Kahn-Freund, C. Lévy and B. Rudden's *Source-book on French Law*, 2nd edn (Clarendon Press, 1979): 'L'expression de "tribunaux judiciaires" peut paraître un pléonasme; elle se justifie pour permettre de qualifier certains tribunaux par opposition aux juridictions administratives. Mais les uns et les autres sont des tribunaux, des juridictions. Lorsque le Conseil d'État statue au contentieux, il est tout autant un tribunal que le tribunal de grande instance ou la Cour d'appel; seulement, c'est un tribunal d'un autre ordre de juridictions.'

party, in which event it is the *juridictions de l'ordre administratif* ('administrative courts') that have exclusive jurisdiction. (In England, of course, all the courts have full jurisdiction to decide cases in administrative matters and to exercise control over administrative bodies and tribunals.[3]) Strictly speaking, the administrative courts belong to the executive arm of the State, so to the French legal mind it is only the *juridictions de l'ordre judiciaire* which are truly part of the *pouvoir judiciaire* or, in the words of the title of Part VIII of the 1958 Constitution, *autorité judiciaire* ('judicial power' or, in some contexts, 'judiciary'), and it is generally only these courts the French lawyer thinks of when discussing the 'judicial' system. The expression *juridictions de l'ordre judiciaire*, which, as Waline observes in his comment quoted in note 2 on p. 67 above, may seem tautologous even in French, is frequently translated as 'the judicial courts' – which, however, is an absurd tautology in English, against a different background. It would therefore seem better to translate the term as 'ordinary courts', although such a translation is scarcely transparent in meaning: but then no translation of the term has very much obvious meaning until it is put in context alongside 'administrative courts', unless one uses 'non-administrative courts' – but that would not be wholly accurate, as there are non-administrative courts which do not belong to the *ordre judiciaire* either (see Sections 6.8 and 6.9), and it would moreover imply that the administrative courts were the norm in some way.[4]

The division between administrative and ordinary courts appears

3. But cf. Lord Denning, writing as far back as 1949: 'It would seem that the French system of administrative courts is worthy of more respect from people in this country than it has sometimes received. So far from granting privileges and immunities to public authorities, the French administrative courts keep them in order and exercise a supervision and control over them which is more complete than anything we have here. These courts have the confidence of the administration because they are staffed by men who understand the administrative problems: and they have the confidence of the public because they are independent of the administration and have proved themselves vigilant to protect the interests of the individual. [. . .] The lesson which can be learnt from the French system is that a separate set of courts dealing with administrative law is not necessarily a threat to the liberty of the individual, but may actually afford him much-needed protection.' Sir Alfred Denning, *Freedom under the Law* (Stevens & Sons, 1949), pp. 79–80.

4. The expressions *juridictions de l'ordre judiciaire* and *juridictions de l'ordre administratif* are sometimes replaced by *la juridiction judiciaire* and *la juridiction administrative* respectively, where *juridiction* is used in its collective sense as an uncountable noun meaning 'jurisdiction'. Note that the normal French word denoting the jurisdiction of a single court is *ressort* (especially geographical or monetary jurisdiction) or *compétence* (legal jurisdiction), though the word *juridiction* is occasionally used in the latter sense – see *plénitude de juridiction* in note 7 below and the discussion of the jurisdiction of the administrative courts on p. 87 below.

to be far more important than the one – to be discussed shortly – between French civil and criminal courts, the *cour d'assises* being in practice, as was mentioned in Section 4.4, the only court in France with an exclusively criminal jurisdiction. The dichotomy also appears to be more fundamental than the major English division of courts into civil and criminal. There is indeed nothing comparable in the English judicial system.

The jurisdictions of the administrative and ordinary courts correspond broadly to the branches of administrative (i.e. public) law and private law respectively. But it is important to appreciate that this correspondence is not a hard-and-fast one: many disputes to which the State is a party – and which accordingly fall within the domain of public law – are within the jurisdiction of the ordinary courts, to which they are often remitted by statute. Such matters include most indirect taxation, expropriation and road accidents involving publicly owned vehicles. Even where there is no statute remitting a given matter involving a State agency to the jurisdiction of the ordinary courts, the administrative courts will not automatically have jurisdiction unless there is some additional special reason to justify the application of administrative-law rules. Moreover, administrative courts may have to refer to private law. Conversely, there are situations in which civil and criminal courts are called upon to apply public law, e.g. when a criminal court, on a preliminary plea of illegality (*exception d'illégalité*), is called upon to decide whether or not a regulation under which someone is being prosecuted is valid; or when an individual seeks redress for a *voie de fait* – a flagrantly unlawful physical act by the authorities which is manifestly outside their powers and infringes a fundamental freedom or a property right.[5]

Finally, cutting across the major dichotomy of administrative versus non-administrative in the French system of courts is a further distinction between *juridictions* (or *tribunaux*) *de droit commun* and *juridictions* (or *tribunaux*) *d'exception*. Although the difference does, as it were, go to jurisdiction, it is essentially a *post factum* distinction of classification rather than a matter of principle. The precise nature of the distinction differs according to which of two meanings is imparted to the term *juridiction d'exception*, but in both cases is related to the distinction between *droit commun* and *loi d'exception* discussed in Section 4.6.

Juridictions d'exception are either (in the more widely known, less technical sense) special (criminal) courts or courts of special (criminal)

5. In criminal law, however, a *voie de fait* is an assault.

jurisdiction – e.g. the *cour d'assises spéciale*, for trying (primarily) terrorist crimes, or the *tribunaux aux armées* ('military courts', 'courts martial'), for trying all offences committed by soldiers serving outside France – and can be so translated; or, in a broader but technically more accurate sense, all specialised courts or courts of limited, statutory jurisdiction – including, among the ordinary courts, the *tribunaux de commerce*, the *tribunaux pour enfants* and, notably, the *tribunaux d'instance* (exercising their civil jurisdiction) and, in the administrative hierarchy, various professional disciplinary bodies and the *Cour des comptes*.[6] In this sense the term can be translated as 'specialised courts' or 'courts of limited jurisdiction'.

Juridictions de droit commun are ordinary courts in the sense of those which ordinarily have jurisdiction, i.e. have jurisdiction – civil, criminal or administrative – to try all cases other than those for which some other court (a *juridiction d'exception*) has been given special jurisdiction by statute.[7] They thus comprise the *tribunaux de grande instance*, the *tribunaux de police* (which exercise the criminal jurisdiction of the *tribunaux d'instance*), the *cours d'assises*, the *cours d'appel*, the *Cour de cassation* and the *tribunaux administratifs*. The term *juridiction de droit commun* could therefore be straightforwardly translated as 'ordinary court', were it not for the fact that this term has already been proposed as the translation of *juridiction de l'ordre judiciaire*. Yet the meanings of the two French terms are different, and the conceptual contrast between *juridictions de droit commun* (which include the *tribunaux administratifs*[8]) and *juridictions d'exception* is not the same as that between *juridictions de l'ordre judiciaire* (which do *not* include the *tribunaux administratifs*) and *juridictions de l'ordre administratif*: *juridictions de droit commun* and *juridictions de l'ordre judiciaire* are 'ordinary courts' in quite different senses. 'Regular court' (offered by Doucet for *juridiction de droit commun*) does not clarify the distinction – and has the drawback of implying that there may be irregular (kangaroo?) courts. For want of any obviously better term, 'ordinary courts' will do as a rendering of

6. In this meaning such courts are referred to in administrative procedure as *juridictions d'attribution*.

7. This should not be confused with the separate concept of having full or unlimited jurisdiction to try questions of law and fact, which is termed *plénitude de juridiction* or (*pouvoir de*) *pleine juridiction*, though these expressions are occasionally used loosely as synonyms for *compétence de droit commun* ('ordinary jurisdiction', i.e. the jurisdiction of the ordinary courts).

8. At the risk of creating confusion, it should be pointed out for the sake of completeness that specialists in public law commonly use the term *juridictions de droit commun* to mean *juridictions de l'ordre judiciaire*.

juridictions de droit commun wherever the context makes it clear that they are being contrasted with *juridictions d'exception* in the sense of 'special courts'; but in cases where the term is contrasted with *juridictions d'exception* in the sense of 'specialised courts' or 'courts of limited jurisdiction', or where it is not clear from the context which sense of *juridiction d'exception* it is being contrasted with, it would perhaps be better translated as 'general courts' or, more explicitly, 'courts of general jurisdiction'.

6.3 Status and titles of judges

Strictly speaking, only the professional judges of the ordinary (non-administrative) courts have the status of *magistrat*,[9] i.e. are members of the *magistrature*, for which the Ministry of Justice is responsible. The judges of the administrative courts are simply *juges* in the generic sense of 'judges' and, in keeping with what was said above about the administrative courts being part of the executive, are civil servants – appointed by the Ministry of the Interior in the case of the first-instance courts and by the Ministry of Justice in the case of the *Conseil d'État* – and therefore technically removable from their posts.[10] As exceptions to this general rule, however, the judges of the *Cour des comptes* and the *chambres régionales des comptes* have had the status of *magistrat* – and thus of irremovability – conferred on them by statute; and the judges of all the administrative courts, including the *Conseil d'État*, are also occasionally referred to, even in legislation, as *magistrats (de l'ordre administratif)* in a broader sense (this generic sense of the term is further exemplified in note 26 on p. 116 below).

While all the judges of the ordinary courts have the status of *magistrat*, however, a distinction of rank is made between those of the higher, appellate courts (i.e. *cours d'appel* and the *Cour de cassation*), who are called *conseillers* ('appeal-court judges', 'judges of appeal', 'judges of the Court of . . .') – which is the title also given to the judges of most administrative courts[11] – and those of the lower, first-instance courts, who are called *juges* ('judges') in a

9. As provided for in Part VIII (*L'autorité judiciaire*) of the Constitution; the precise meaning of this term is discussed in Section 7.2.

10. From January 1990, however, the staff of the *tribunaux administratifs* – and of the new administrative courts of appeal (see Section 6.7 below) – will be part of a single *corps* coming under the Secretary-General of the *Conseil d'État*.

11. In the *Conseil d'État*, *conseiller (d'État)* is the senior rank in the internal hierarchy – see Section 6.7. below.

specific sense. (The judges of the *cour d'assises*, being drawn both from the *cour d'appel* and from the first-instance *tribunal de grande instance*, will be *conseillers* or *juges*, as the case may be.)

6.4 The *Cour de cassation* and the ordinary courts of first instance

The ordinary (non-administrative) courts are headed by the *Cour de cassation*, which is the supreme court of the *ordre judiciaire*. Its structure and function will be described in more detail in Section 6.5, but broadly speaking it is a court of final appeal on questions of law and exercises ultimate supervision over all the courts which apply private law (including criminal law and social-security law). Unlike English courts of appeal, however, it does not usually substitute its own decision for a lower court's judgment with which it disagrees, but merely sets aside or quashes the judgment ('quash' and *casser* are cognates) and remits the case for rehearing by another court of the same rank as the one which gave the original judgment. In 1987 it disposed of over 25,000 cases.

Since there is no equivalent appeal procedure in English law (although analogies will be suggested later), a functionally equivalent translation of *Cour de cassation* is impossible; but, given that the term 'cassation' has long existed in English (as was noted in passing in Section 2.6), there seems to be no reason why the term should not be translated word for word as 'Court of Cassation'. But if that rendering is felt to be insufficiently transparent in meaning or so unfamiliar and uninformative to the average English lawyer or other reader of the translation as to be no more helpful than the original French and to require a gloss, one may as well keep the original term and provide a gloss. At all events, 'Supreme Court (of Appeal)' is unsuitable as a translation, given the two hierarchies of the French court system, both of which have their own supreme courts. (And in England, of course, the so-called Supreme Court of Judicature, consisting of the High Court and the Court of Appeal, is not a final appellate body, the supreme court being the House of Lords.)

That much having been said about the Court of Cassation by way of introduction, let us now consider the hierarchy of ordinary courts in logical order from the bottom upwards.

The lowest court in the hierarchy – with a jurisdiction combining roughly that of a magistrates' court and a county court in England, i.e. limited primary jurisdiction – is the *tribunal d'instance*, which is

Diagram 6.1 The French courts

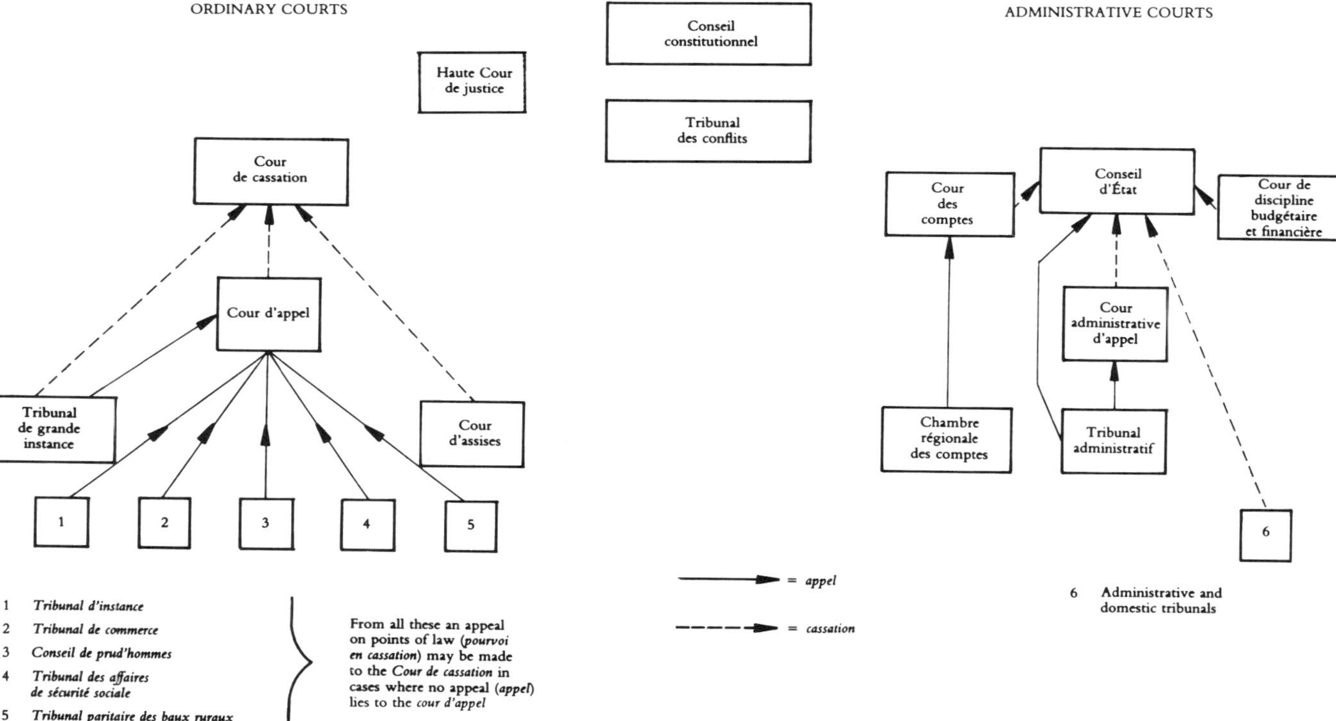

the only court in France to sit as such with a single judge[12] and has a geographical jurisdiction corresponding to the *arrondissement* (a subdivision of a *département*). When exercising its criminal jurisdiction it is referred to as the *tribunal de police*, the two courts being staffed by the same judges, who are seconded from the *tribunal de grande instance* (to be mentioned in a moment) and, like English county-court judges but unlike most magistrates, are paid professionals; in Paris, Lyons and Marseilles, however, there are separate *tribunaux de police* independent of the *tribunaux d'instance*.

Given that the two terms exist, corresponding exactly to the civil and criminal jurisdictions, it is not possible to translate either of them as, say, 'county court' or 'magistrates' court' – the functional differences are simply too great. Unlike the *tribunal d'instance* and the *tribunal de police*, county courts and magistrates' courts are quite different things: they are staffed by different kinds of judge, and appeal from them lies to different courts. Moreover, county courts can try cases where the sums in dispute are much larger than those for which the *tribunal d'instance* has jurisdiction (£5,000 in contract and tort and up to £30,000 in equity, as against 30,000 francs – and the county-court figures are likely to be increased soon under the Courts and Legal Services Bill to be put before Parliament); while magistrates' courts have a mixed jurisdiction, albeit primarily a criminal one.

Tribunal de police can readily be translated as 'police court' – a word-for-word rendering which has the merit of being fairly transparent in meaning and of having actually existed as the old name for a magistrates' court (which is the nearest equivalent in the English system in terms of level of jurisdiction, even if too different for its name to be used as a translation).

The problem of translating *tribunal d'instance*, however, is more intractable. Doucet's amazing 'tribunal of instance' must clearly be ruled out of court, as it were, at the outset; while the term used by Michael Kindred[13] – 'Court of Minor Jurisdiction' – is at best a definition and is inconceivable as a title of a court in England. The only possibility seems to be the rendering suggested by Bridge: 'district court', by analogy with 'county court' (which are in any case 'county' courts in name only, being in reality district courts

12. Most French courts are constituted of benches of at least three judges. Some jurisdictions of courts, however, are exercised – or are exercisable in certain circumstances – by a single judge (e.g. the *juge des enfants*, discussed on p. 77 below).

13. The translator of the French original of René David's *French Law. Its Structure, Sources, and Methodology* (Louisiana State University Press, 1972).

almost as numerous as the *tribunaux d'instance*). Like most translations based purely on a court's territorial jurisdiction (e.g. 'Regional Court'), however, this term gives no clue to the precise function or legal jurisdiction of the *tribunal d'instance* and could, moreover, apply equally well to other, specialised courts of similar territorial jurisdiction, although admittedly a court will usually be assumed to have a general competence if its name does not indicate a specialised one. (It could also confuse a Scottish lawyer, as the district courts in Scotland, while being the lowest courts, have only criminal jurisdiction and are staffed by mostly lay magistrates.) It may well sometimes be preferable, therefore, to transcribe the French term and gloss it as appropriate to the context of its use; but 'district court' is the translation that will be adopted in this book.

Where sums larger than 30,000 francs are involved in civil actions or where the more serious offences (*délits*[14]) are being tried in criminal cases, the competent court is the *tribunal de grande instance*, usually situated in the chief town or city of each *département*, although the more populous *départements* have two or more of these courts. Writers are frequently tempted to equate the *tribunal de grande instance* with the English High Court, but the analogy is inaccurate[15] and therefore the translation 'High Court' is unacceptable in any but a text intended for the general reader.[16] The *tribunal de grande instance* is the normal court of first instance in civil matters (i.e. except for the small claims dealt with in the *tribunal d'instance*) and thus corresponds more to the English county court. But it is also a court of first instance in criminal matters, with a jurisdiction not unlike that of the old Quarter Sessions in England. In England, however, all criminal cases start life in the magistrates' court, even if the accused may subsequently be committed for trial at the Crown Court. The High Court's jurisdiction, on the other hand, is primarily civil, and in both civil and criminal cases it has appellate jurisdiction, whereas the *tribunal de grande instance* has none. Finally, the jurisdiction of the *tribunaux de grande instance* is decentralised, there being 175 of them in metropolitan France, whereas the High Court, though represented in large provincial cities by a district registrar and statutorily able to sit anywhere in England and Wales, has its seat in London and conducts most of its business there.

The *tribunaux de grande instance* are in effect county courts with

14. For the classification of criminal offences in France see Section 8.1.

15. Quite apart from the fact that 'High Court' could in theory be confused with the *Haute Cour de justice*, to be mentioned later.

16. 'The High Court of Bordeaux [etc.]' has none the less been used in law reports in *The Times*.

criminal as well as unlimited civil original jurisdiction, and their name is therefore really untranslatable – in fact one of the very few untranslatable terms that will be encountered in this study. Professor Walker in his *Oxford Companion to Law* curiously refers to 'Courts of Grand Instance', which is reminiscent of Doucet's rendering of *tribunal d'instance* and must similarly be rejected out of hand as meaningless. Kindred predictably – and at least with the merit of consistency – offers the definition-translation 'Court of Major Jurisdiction'. Bridge gives 'regional court', but this term is as vague as 'district court' and even more unacceptable as it could equally well be applied to, say, a *tribunal administratif. Tribunal de grande instance* must accordingly be transcribed and glossed as appropriate.

The criminal jurisdiction of the Tribunal de Grande Instance is exercised by its *chambre correctionnelle*, often referred to as the *tribunal correctionnel* (which can conveniently be rendered as 'Criminal Court'; Doucet's and O'Rooney's 'correctional court' is a Gallicism devoid of meaning in this context, since, in so far as 'correctional' is used at all in English, it describes prison institutions of one kind or another). A word is necessary about the translation of *chambre*, however, which is the standard French term used to denote any permanent or *ad hoc* section of any court as opposed to the whole body of judges belonging to the court in question. For some undiscoverable reason this term is invariably translated as 'chamber', as it is with reference to the European Court of Human Rights, for instance.[17] Yet it is surely clear that a permanently constituted section of a court (like the *chambre correctionnelle*) is in English called a 'division' (e.g. the Criminal Division of the Court of Appeal or the Chancery Division of the High Court); while an *ad hoc* group of judges (as in the European Court of Human Rights) is usually referred to as a 'court' (as in 'a court of three' or 'a full court') or a 'bench' (of magistrates particularly), though also occasionally as a 'division' (e.g. 'the case had been heard by a different division of the Court of Appeal'). Another possibility in certain contexts would be 'panel' (as in the 'juvenile panel' of a magistrates' court). It should be unnecessary to add that 'chamber' is in any case a bad translation on two grounds: firstly, the term is commonly associated with the collocations 'chamber of commerce' and 'the Upper/Lower Chamber'; and secondly, in the legal field it is familiar in the expressions 'barristers' chambers' and – potentially most confusing of all – 'judge sitting in chambers'. *Chambre correctionnelle* should

17. See Article 43 of the European Convention on Human Rights (1950).

clearly be translated as '(the) Criminal Division (of the Tribunal de Grande Instance)'.

A further section of the Tribunal de Grande Instance is the *tribunal pour enfants* ('Juvenile Court'), which counts as a *juridiction d'exception* in the sense of being a specialised court. It consists of a judge appointed for three years at a time from the Tribunal de Grande Instance and two lay assessors. It exercises both criminal and civil jurisdiction over children under 18, though cases of serious crime – *crime*[18] – committed by children aged 16 or 17 are heard by the *cour d'assises des mineurs*, to be mentioned shortly. The presiding judge is known as the *juge des enfants* ('Juvenile Court judge'), who in less serious matters (in terms of attracting a lesser penalty) can sit without assessors. This jurisdiction (or one broadly corresponding to it) is exercised in England by magistrates' courts.

Cases of serious crime are tried by the *cour d'assises* ('Assize Court', 'Court of Assize', 'Assizes'). There is an assize court in each *département*, but it ordinarily sits only once every quarter. Assize courts are composed of three judges (the presiding judge being a member of the *cour d'appel*[19] and the other two judges coming from either that court or the Tribunal de Grande Instance) sitting with nine lay *jurés* ('jurors'; *les jurés* – 'the jury'), all of whom, deliberating together, decide questions of law and fact and determine any sentence to be passed, by a majority (a majority of at least eight being required for any decision – other than the sentence itself – unfavourable to the accused). When trying young persons of 16 or 17 who commit serious crimes, the court is constituted as a *cour d'assises des mineurs* ('Assize Court for Juveniles' or perhaps 'Juvenile Assize Court'), with an ordinary jury but with two of the three judges being specialists in juvenile cases, usually Juvenile Court judges.

Since 1982 there has been within the territorial jurisdiction of each *cour d'appel* a *cour d'assises spéciale* or *spécialement composée* ('special Assize Court') to try treason, espionage and other national-security cases and the most serious civil or military offences (*crimes*)[20] committed by soldiers serving in France. This special court replaced another *juridiction d'exception*, the *Cour de sûreté de l'État* ('National Security Court'), abolished in 1981, and its

18. See Section 8.1.

19. See Section 6.5.

20. Other serious offences (*délits*) committed by soldiers serving in France are tried by a specially designated Tribunal de Grande Instance within the territorial jurisdiction of each *cour d'appel*.

jurisdiction was extended in 1986 to include terrorist crimes. It is composed of seven judges sitting without a jury.

The courts mentioned so far are all ordinary courts of first instance, in the sense of not being administrative courts, and (except for the *tribunal d'instance*, the juvenile courts, the special Assize Court and the military courts) are also courts of general jurisdiction. Mention must also be made, however, of the other principal ordinary courts of first instance, which are all specialised or special courts.

Of these the longest standing are the *tribunaux de commerce*, of which there are nearly 230. They consist of three lay *juges consulaires* ('commercial judges'), who have all been in commerce themselves for at least five years and are elected by their peers in the form of an electoral college consisting of traders' delegates. They hear all disputes relating to commercial transactions and bankruptcy. The presiding judge has powers similar to those of the presiding judge of the Tribunal de Grande Instance – which hears commercial cases in areas where there is no *tribunal de commerce*.[21] The jurisdiction of the Commercial Court set up within the Queen's Bench Division of the High Court in England in 1970 is sufficiently similar – or, alternatively, the label 'commercial court' is sufficiently general – for the term to be usable as a translation of *tribunal de commerce* (or *juridiction consulaire*, as it is sometimes called).

The other main specialised civil courts are all what in England would be termed 'tribunals' (cf. Section 6.1 above), and the word 'court' should accordingly not be used in translating their names.

Social-security disputes are heard at first instance by the *tribunaux des affaires de sécurité sociale*,[22] of which there are 110, each consisting of two lay assessors appointed by the President of the Tribunal de Grande Instance – one representing employees and one representing employers and the self-employed – and presided over by a judge from the Tribunal de Grande Instance. As these tribunals are similar to the English social-security appeal tribunals, the French term can be rendered simply as 'social-security appeal tribunal'.

Employment disputes are determined by the *conseils de prud'hommes*, of which there are at least one in each *département* and over 280 in all. These tribunals have five divisions (corresponding

21. In Alsace-Lorraine there are no separate courts at all for trying commercial cases, which are heard by special divisions (*chambres commerciales*) of the local Tribunaux de Grande Instance composed of one professional judge (the Vice-President of the Tribunal), who presides, and two elected traders.

22. Until 1985 these tribunals were called *commissions de première instance de sécurité sociale*.

to different sectors of employment), each of which comprises at least three elected representatives of employees and three of employers, in equal numbers. These divisions (*sections*) may in turn be subdivided into *chambres* (here perhaps best translated as 'section' rather than 'panel', to avoid confusion with the *bureaux* to be mentioned in a moment). The *conseils* have a dual function of conciliation and adjudication and accordingly sit in two different compositions. Firstly, there is a *bureau de conciliation* ('conciliation panel'), before which all litigants must initially appear and which is composed of two assessors (one employee and one employer). Secondly, there is a *bureau de jugement* ('adjudication panel'), which determines cases in which conciliation has proved impossible and is composed of two employee assessors and two employer assessors. In the event of an even split of opinion, the case is reheard with the additional presence of a judge from the district court, who will preside. Two assessors sitting alone and acting for all the divisions jointly may also hear urgent interlocutory applications '*en référé*' (cf. English judges sitting in chambers); again, a judge from the district court will be called in if the assessors cannot agree.[23]

Many different translations have been proposed for *conseil de prud'hommes*. In so far as these tribunals are clearly the French equivalent of English industrial tribunals, there is much to be said for translating the term accordingly. 'Labour Court' is un-English-sounding – and 'court' is in any case inappropriate (the short-lived National Industrial Relations Court in England was, as the name makes clear, a national court, not a local tribunal). Alternatively, 'employment tribunal' could be used (similarly sounding better than 'labour tribunal' – but possibly risking confusion with the English Employment Appeal Tribunal, a national appellate court). The fact that the French name uses the word *conseil* is no argument for using the English term 'council' or 'board': the French bodies clearly have a judicial function, and this must be indicated; Kindred's translation 'labour boards' must therefore be rejected. 'Tribunal' is plainly the right term – the decisions of the *conseils* are binding – but how should it be qualified? The medieval and now otherwise archaic French word *prud'homme* means a man of loyalty and integrity – and the *conseils de prud'hommes* are, as has been explained, under a duty in the first instance to seek a settlement

23. A judge known as the *juge des référés* is vested with similar powers to hear urgent applications (summarily but *inter partes*) in other first-instance courts too, notably the Tribunal de Grande Instance and the Commercial Court, whose presidents exercise the power.

of the disputes brought before them. Accordingly, the translation 'labour conciliation tribunal' used in the Council of Europe's *Judicial Organisation in Europe* is a good suggestion. Since the word 'labour' is not used in the title of any English judicial body, however, 'industrial conciliation tribunal' would ultimately seem to be the best translation.

Finally, in the category of tribunals, the 400-odd *tribunaux paritaires des baux ruraux* determine agrarian landlord-and-tenant disputes. These tribunals, of which there is one attached to most of the district courts, consist of four elected assessors – two landlords (who are not also tenants) and two tenants (who are not also landlords) – presided over by a judge of the district court. It is unnecessary – and would sound incongruous – to translate *paritaire* in the English title (and the French word is not used in the names *tribunal des affaires de sécurité sociale* and *conseil de prud'hommes*, which likewise both have equal numbers of representatives from the relevant two 'sides' in the disputes they hear). The Council of Europe manual's literal translation 'Court for rural leases' sounds most improbable as a title for a tribunal in English, while Doucet gives only a lengthy definition instead of a translation. The English agricultural land tribunals are sufficiently similar in function, composition and jurisdiction for the functionally equivalent translation 'agricultural land tribunal' to be acceptable, and this indeed is the rendering suggested by Bridge.

It is perhaps worth noting at this point that there is a generic term *juridiction échevinale* to describe courts like the *tribunal des affaires de sécurité sociale* and the *cour d'assises*, which are composed of one or more professional judges sitting with lay assessors or jurors. 'Court sitting with assessors/a jury' or 'court which sits with assessors/a jury' is a satisfactory rendering of *juridiction échevinale* where the French term is in the singular, but would have to be amended to 'courts . . . with assessors or a jury' in the plural. The principle of having this mixed composition is known as *échevinage*.

The last court to be mentioned in this section is a special criminal court established by the 1958 Constitution but which has existed in one form or another under all previous constitutions: the *Haute Cour de justice*. The twenty-four judges of the present-day court are elected by the National Assembly and the Senate in equal numbers from among their own members after each parliamentary election, and the court has jurisdiction, upon impeachment by both Houses separately, to try the President of the Republic for high treason and government ministers (and, in the case of conspiracy against the State, their accomplices) for any serious offences (*crimes* or *délits*) committed in the course of their duties. The court is in fact a court of both first and last instance, as no appeal lies against its judgments. It is, obviously, a political court and in that sense lies outside the two hierarchies of ordinary and administrative courts; but it is normally included in any account of the ordinary courts, as it applies the ordinary criminal law and procedure in force at the time of the alleged offences.

There would seem to be only two possible ways of dealing with the translation of this court's title, given that there is no functional equivalent of the court in England. Either, on the basis that the quite different English High Court is usually so called rather than referred to by its full title 'High Court of Justice', it may be translated as 'High Court of Justice'; or else, if the risk of confusion seems too great (at least in a given context), the French title must be transcribed and glossed.

6.5 Appellate ordinary courts

From all the courts of first instance discussed so far except the Assize Court[24] and the High Court of Justice appeal (*appel*[25]) lies either unconditionally or conditionally (e.g. in civil cases involving more than a specified sum or in criminal cases in which the sentence passed exceeds a specified level of fine or term of imprisonment) to the *cour d'appel*. This is again a decentralised jurisdiction – a regional one, there being thirty such courts in metropolitan France – but its function and name are so similar to those of the English Court of Appeal that any translation other than 'court of appeal' is really unthinkable except perhaps in unlikely contexts where there is any risk of confusion with the English court.

On the civil side, courts of appeal have one or more divisions of at least one of the following types: a *chambre civile* ('Civil Division'), which hears appeals from the civil divisions of the Tribunal de Grande Instance and the district court, from the agricultural land

24. No appeal lies from the Assize Court because, unlike the other criminal courts, it sits with a jury, whose verdict is regarded as being irrefragable (though a retrial will often be ordered if the original verdict is set aside by the Court of Cassation on purely legal grounds – see p. 82 and note 26 below).

25. This is only one possible form of appeal – on questions of both law and fact – and the French word is correspondingly narrower in meaning than its English formal equivalent 'appeal'. In addition to the other modes of appeal discussed on pp. 82–6 below, *opposition* ('an application to set aside') may be made (to most courts of first instance) in respect of judgments given in default or *in absentia*.

tribunals and, if there is no separate division for the purpose, from the commercial courts; a *chambre sociale* ('Social Division'), which hears appeals from the social-security appeal tribunals and the industrial conciliation tribunals; and a *chambre commerciale* ('Commercial Division'), which hears appeals from the commercial courts. On the criminal side, appeals are usually heard by a *chambre des appels correctionnels* ('Criminal Division'), except for those involving a minor, which are heard by the *chambre des mineurs* ('Juvenile Division').

Courts of appeal also have another, rather different criminal division known as the *chambre d'accusation*. This division has a variety of functions. Its principal duties relate to the pre-trial stages of criminal cases rather than consisting in rehearing cases already tried: it hears appeals against orders made by *juges d'instruction* (see Section 8.4) – notably against pre-trial detention orders – and decides whether cases of serious crime are to be sent for trial at the Assizes, in which capacity it acts rather like the former grand juries in England, although the *chambre d'accusation* has no jury but, like the other divisions of the court, sits as a court of three judges. Other functions include supervising extradition, rehabilitation and amnesties and acting as the disciplinary body of the police (criminal-investigation officers). Since the division's French title refers only to the function of committing persons for trial at the Assize Court, there is no reason why it should not simply be translated in English as 'Indictment Division'.

From decisions of courts of appeal, from final – i.e. unappealable – decisions of all the courts of first instance from which appeal (*appel*) would in other circumstances lie and, lastly, from the Assize Court[26] a different form of appeal is available, on points of law only, to the supreme Court of Cassation. Such an appeal is known as a *pourvoi en cassation* (or occasionally as a *recours en cassation*). Before consideration is given to how this term is to be translated, it will be helpful to describe briefly the working of the Court of Cassation.

The court currently has five civil divisions – three of which are called the first, second and third *chambres civiles* ('civil divisions') respectively, one the *chambre commerciale et financière* ('Commercial and Financial Division') and one the *chambre sociale* ('Social Divi-

26. Whereas courts of appeal not only make findings both of law and of fact but can also reverse acquittals on appeal in criminal cases, an acquittal by an assize court can be reviewed by the Court of Cassation only in the interests of the law and without prejudice to the party acquitted.

sion') – and a *chambre criminelle* ('Criminal Division'). Cases are heard by a minimum of three (usually five) judges from a single division, and there are over a hundred judges in all, including the *premier président* ('President'), the *présidents* (*de chambre*) (each of which could be referred to as 'President of the . . . Division' or 'president of a division of the Court of Cassation'), over 80 *conseillers* (*à la Cour de cassation*) ('judges of the Court of Cassation') and some two dozen *conseillers référendaires*,[27] who were originally purely advisory judges seconded to the court on account of special expertise but since 1978 have also been able to vote in certain circumstances, notably in cases for which they have been the reporting judge; their title could be translated as 'auxiliary judges'. Finally, a new category of staff – the *auditeurs* (*à la Cour de cassation*) – was created in 1984. Its members have purely administrative and support duties and their title may be translated as 'administrative assistants'.

Cases which raise particularly important issues of law, especially ones affecting more than one division of the court, or issues on which a conflict of opinion is apparent between earlier decisions of different divisions are heard by a minimum of thirteen judges from three or more divisions sitting as a *chambre mixte* presided over by the President of the court. Since the *chambre mixte* is an *ad hoc* body, the term *chambre* cannot here be translated as 'division', and the expression would seem best rendered as a 'mixed bench' – or perhaps 'joint bench' or 'composite bench' if 'mixed bench' is thought to be phonetically too reminiscent of 'mixed bunch'.

It was pointed out at the beginning of Section 6.4 that successful applications to the Court of Cassation result in the lower court's decision being quashed and the case being remitted to another court of the same rank as the one whose judgment has been set aside (or to the original court differently constituted). This lower court, however, is not bound to accept the Court of Cassation's view of the law; and if it declines to do so and its decision is in its turn appealed to the Court of Cassation on the same legal grounds as before, that court will sit as an *assemblée plénière* (or *en banc*, formerly *en chambres réunies*) – a 'full court' of twenty-five judges from all six divisions will be convened by the President of the court.[28] If the court again quashes the lower court's decision on the

27. This is also the title of middle-ranking members of the *Cour des comptes* (for which see Section 6.6).

28. Cases can also be referred direct to the full court by a joint bench or even by an ordinary bench (in which case the court's judgment will, if the lower court's

same grounds as before, it will either remit the case to a third lower court, which will then be bound by the Court of Cassation's view of the law, or it may (though in criminal cases only to a limited extent) decide the case itself if it has enough facts and evidence at its disposal. Since 1979 it has also been similarly possible for a case to be determined on its merits after the original decision has been quashed for the first time; and there have always been occasions, frequent in criminal cases, when for purely technical reasons – e.g. because an amnesty has been declared or the original appeal was out of time – a case has not been remitted for retrial in the first place.

Given this procedure, what is the best way of translating *pourvoi en cassation*? The *pourvoi* is in fact an application to a higher court to have a judgment set aside on legal grounds, and as such has no real equivalent in English law. There is accordingly no neat or exact functionally equivalent translation. On the other hand, the Court of Cassation's function strongly resembles that of the Queen's Bench Divisional Court when hearing an 'appeal by way of case stated' from a magistrates' court or a Crown Court, the principal difference being that the Queen's Bench Divisional Court, unlike the Court of Cassation (except in the circumstances mentioned), frequently determines the merits of the particular case as well as the law before remitting it to the *original* magistrates' court, which must then act as directed by the Divisional Court – whether by applying the law as stated by the Divisional Court and reaching its own conclusion on the merits or, say, complying with a specific direction to convict or acquit a defendant. There are also similarities between a *pourvoi en cassation* and the English 'application for judicial review', in which the Divisional Court is asked to review the legality of an administrative body's – or, less often, an inferior court's – proceedings and/or decision. In such proceedings, though, cases are often not remitted to the original court (or other decision-making authority) at all, the Divisional Court substituting its own decision; and such applications are probably nowadays more frequently directed against an administrative decision than against a court or tribunal decision (and are thus not appeals in the narrow, judicial sense). In his *Civil Law and the Anglo-American Lawyer* Henry de Vries uses the translation 'petition for review', and either that or 'application for review' would seem at first sight

decision is quashed, be binding straightaway on the court to which the case may be remitted). The *assemblée plénière* should not be confused with the *assemblée générale* ('General Assembly') of all the court's judges, which is convened for administrative or advisory purposes.

to be the nearest rendering, while having the merit of being sufficiently non-specific for the differences in procedure not to matter. A better translation, however, is 'appeal on points of law', which, although not strictly a functional equivalent, is more exact and leaves open the possibility of using 'judicial review' in its wider sense to translate *contrôle judiciaire/juridictionnel*. 'Judicial review' in its narrower sense is in any event primarily a form of appeal against administrative action – which in France is challengeable only in the separate administrative courts to be described shortly.[29] An alternative translation – perhaps the simplest – would be 'application to the Court of Cassation', but that does not have the advantage of at least suggesting what is involved, unless the reader is already familiar with the function of the Court of Cassation (and see note 40 on p. 91 below).

Before we leave the ordinary courts in general and the Court of Cassation and the subject of appeals in particular, mention should be made lastly of another, exceptional form of appeal, *révision*. In criminal cases which have been finally disposed of judicially, a convicted defendant or the Minister of Justice may in certain limited circumstances lodge a *pourvoi en révision* with the Court of Cassation, alleging wrongful conviction and petitioning the court to order a fresh hearing of the case.[30] There is no equivalent formal procedure in English law (though the Home Secretary has the power to refer cases to the Court of Appeal if significant new evidence has come to light), and consequently no functionally equivalent translation is possible. Although the term *révision* literally means 'review', this word-for-word translation is likely to cause confusion with the quite different English remedy of 'judicial review'. A semantically (but non-functionally) equivalent translation is therefore called for, and 'application for a retrial' would seem to be the simplest and most idiomatic-sounding. In civil cases which have acquired the force of *res judicata* a *recours en révision* (formerly a *requête civile*) may be made on a very limited number of grounds to the original trial court itself, which may agree to rehear the case and/or alter its decision. Again, there is no equivalent of this procedure in English law, and a semantically equivalent translation

29. Furthermore, as L. N. Brown and J. F. Garner point out in their book *French Administrative Law*, 3rd edn (Butterworths, 1983), p. 4, 'judicial review' carries a different connotation again in the United States and other parts of the English-speaking world, where it refers to the power of the courts to declare legislation unconstitutional.

30. Perhaps the most celebrated historical instance of such a demand for a new trial – finally granted only after many years' agitation – occurred in the Dreyfus case.

is needed: perhaps 'application to reopen proceedings' would best give an indication of the remedy's exceptional nature while remaining distinct from the renderings suggested for *opposition* and *pourvoi en révision*.

6.6 The *Conseil d'État* and the administrative courts of first instance

It has long been felt in France that the ordinary courts are not suited to considering the special circumstances and factors affecting administrative decisions,[31] and it was accordingly thought desirable to develop a special system of courts inside the *administration*[32] itself, staffed by judges who had some link with it. The principal outcome of this view was the *Conseil d'État*, created in essentially its modern form by Napoleon at the end of 1799. The precise structure and functions of the *Conseil d'État* will be described in detail in the next section, but inasmuch as it is the supreme court of the administrative hierarchy of courts, it stands in much the same relation to the lower administrative courts as the Court of Cassation does to the lower ordinary courts. Clearly there is absolutely no equivalent British institution at all and therefore no possible functionally equivalent translation.[33] The course commonly adopted is to use a word-for-word translation, 'Council of State'. The meaning of that, however, is not only unclear but also misleading, as it gives no hint of any judicial function (admittedly not the *Conseil*'s only function, as will be explained in the next section);

31. The *locus classicus* in which this principle is enshrined is section 13 of the Act of 16–24 August 1790: 'Les fonctions judiciaires sont distinctes et demeureront toujours séparées des fonctions administratives: les juges ne pourront à peine de forfaiture troubler de quelque manière que ce soit les opérations des corps administratifs.'

32. This term is perhaps most accurately rendered as 'the public service': it includes – but is not exclusively composed of – what in England would be termed 'the civil service' and covers all public bodies and services, national and local, except the judiciary (i.e. the judges of the ordinary courts) and other *magistrats* (see Section 7.2). Another possible translation is 'the executive', and in many contexts the term can best be translated simply as 'the authorities'. When the *administration* is being contrasted with the government of the day, the appropriate translation may be 'the bureaucracy'.

33. In an article entitled 'Public and Private Law' in the *Law Society's Gazette* of 23 March 1983, pp. 739–40, Professor Garner, when discussing the increased use of judicial review (referred to at the beginning of Section 4.2), described the Queen's Bench Division as beginning to look like a specialised administrative court. But he added: 'though not on the pattern of the French *Conseil d'État*, as it is staffed by judges and has no important administrative functions' (p. 739).

if anything, such a translation suggests some kind of purely political Cabinet. A more appropriate translation (in terms of semantic equivalence) would be 'Supreme Administrative Court', but this is not really satisfactory either, as it suggests that the *Conseil* has exclusively judicial functions. The only wholly acceptable solution is to transcribe – 'Conseil d'État' – and gloss as appropriate to the context (e.g. as 'the supreme administrative court' or 'national body advising the government on legislation').

The administrative courts as a whole have essentially a dual jurisdiction. Firstly, they exercise the sort of control over the legality of administrative action that is exercised – mainly through the so-called prerogative orders of mandamus, prohibition and certiorari and through declarations – by the Queen's Bench Divisional Court on applications for judicial review, and they have power to annul administrative acts and decisions and also regulations (cf. Section 5.2), this being termed the *juridiction d'annulation* ('annulment jurisdiction').[34] Secondly, they can afford redress in the form of damages to those who have suffered injury or damage as a result of a wrongful act on the part of a public servant acting in the course of his duties,[35] this being termed their *pleine juridiction* ('full jurisdiction'), under which the courts also have power, in appropriate cases, to alter the administrative decision complained of.

Only two categories of executive or administrative act are exempt from review by the administrative courts: those connected directly with, or forming part of, the legislative process and parliamentary proceedings; and those concerning the government's relations with foreign countries or with international organisations (including the validity and interpretation of treaties – though the application of a treaty may raise questions of domestic law, which will be amenable to review).

As in the discussion of the ordinary courts, the lowest tier – the *tribunaux administratifs* ('administrative courts'[36]) – will be considered

34. Statutes have hitherto been immune from review under this jurisdiction – a view upheld by the Conseil d'État in 1968. But in 1975 the Court of Cassation held that a treaty took precedence over a later Act of Parliament, and in 1989 the Conseil d'État at last came round to this view, thus seemingly breaching for the future the immunity of statutes from review, at least in this respect.

35. There are some exceptions, as noted in Section 6.2.

36. This is the same translation as the one offered earlier for *juridictions de l'ordre administratif*, i.e. the administrative courts as a whole – the problem being, once again, the lack of a set of distinctions in English corresponding to *juridiction/tribunal/cour*: 'court' has to do for all three French terms. It will not be often that the

first. These courts of first instance acquired their present name and general jurisdiction at first instance only in 1953, when it was decided that something radical had to be done to reduce the excessive case-load of the Conseil d'État (until then the normal court of first and last instance in administrative matters). They are regional courts – there being 26 of them in metropolitan France – and it is to them that cases involving the public service usually have to be submitted in the first instance, although, as already noted, the ordinary courts have been given jurisdiction in a number of fields, as also have three specialised administrative courts and some forty[37] or so *juridictions administratives* – specialised administrative and, more particularly, domestic (i.e. professional disciplinary) tribunals;[38] and in some matters the Conseil d'État statutorily retains original (and final) jurisdiction, for example in cases concerning the legality of decrees and ministerial regulations, the careers of officials appointed by presidential decree, or administrative decisions whose application extends beyond the territorial jurisdiction of a single administrative court (of first instance).

Actions invoking the annulment jurisdiction are called *recours en annulation pour excès de pouvoir*, usually shortened to *recours en annulation* or (slightly oddly) *recours pour excès de pouvoir.*[39] While *recours en annulation* could be translated as an 'action for annulment' (in the case of an administrative regulation) or 'action to set aside' (in the case of an administrative decision), a *recours pour excès de pouvoir* covers a wider range of grounds for review than just *ultra vires* or excess of powers, and accordingly that term cannot be used in translating *recours pour excès de pouvoir.* Given the synonymy of the French short terms for this action, it seems desirable to translate them (and the full term) identically, and for once there does seem to

---

lowest-tier administrative courts have to be referred to in the plural, however; and where they are, the qualification 'of first instance' can be added.

37. This figure may be compared with the 70-odd tribunals in England, a number reflecting the relatively undeveloped state of English administrative law: the French, having long had a coherent body of administrative law and the prestigious Conseil d'État to apply it, have felt less need to create separate tribunals of limited, specialised jurisdiction.

38. As has been seen, these do not include some tribunals which in England would be regarded as typically administrative but in France apply private law – the social-security, industrial and agricultural land tribunals. Interestingly enough, moreover, the domestic tribunals do not include lawyers' professional disciplinary bodies; thus from a bar council (*conseil de l'ordre des avocats*) appeal lies to the Court of Appeal.

39. The actual document lodged to commence proceedings is strictly called a *requête* ('application').

be an almost exact equivalent in the English system, notwithstanding that there are no separate administrative courts in England. The main point is that such actions in administrative law can be brought in both countries, on not dissimilar grounds and with not dissimilar results; and that being so, there seems no reason why this action should not be translated by the admittedly specific but semantically quite transparent term 'application for judicial review of administrative action' (an action that even in England can in fact only be brought – with leave – in one court, the Queen's Bench Divisional Court, which, as noted above, has become something of a specialised administrative court). In an appropriate context where no misunderstanding is possible (cf. note 29 on p. 85 above), the English term can likewise conveniently be abbreviated, to 'judicial review'.

An action invoking the full jurisdiction of the Administrative Court is known as a *recours de pleine juridiction* or a *recours en indemnité*. These more or less interchangeable terms are usually most helpfully both rendered as 'action for damages (in the administrative courts)', though the purpose of a *recours de pleine juridiction* may be to seek a form of relief fuller than mere damages and in place of them, e.g. in an action in the Conseil d'État to have an election declared invalid, when the court may not only quash the election but recount the votes and declare the rightful candidate elected; in that case a rendering such as simply 'an administrative-law action' might be appropriate.

Alongside the general administrative courts, 24 *chambres régionales des comptes* – including one for each of the 22 mainland administrative regions – were set up in 1983 under an Act passed in 1982. They have both judicial and non-judicial functions. Their judicial duty is to judge all public expenditure at the level of the regions, *départements* and municipalities. At the same time, they exercise administrative supervision of public funds at the same level, not unlike the English district auditors, and can make critical reports. Since these *chambres* are not divisions of a court but are autonomous bodies acting in their own right (like *chambres de commerce* – 'chambers of commerce'), the translations previously suggested for *chambre* would be inappropriate here, and the title of these bodies is probably best rendered in English as 'regional audit boards' – the term used by Brown and Garner in their *French Administrative Law* – or 'regional boards of auditors'.

Against judgments of these boards (exercising their judicial powers) appeal (*appel*) lies to the national *Cour des comptes*. This court, however, has primarily original jurisdiction of a kind similar to that of the regional audit boards, being responsible for auditing the accounts of State treasurers and paymasters at national level and for supervising the carrying out by the appropriate officials of budgetary measures decided by Parliament. In this rôle it may be compared to the British Public Accounts Committee of the House of Commons and the Comptroller and Auditor-General. Since, however, these accounting functions are coupled with judicial powers in that the *Cour des comptes* can order rectification of errors made by the officials it supervises and, in appropriate cases, impose sanctions, the commonly offered translation 'Comptroller and Auditor-General's Department' (or the alternative 'National Audit Office') is not wholly apt, and there is no reason why the word-for-word translation 'Audit Court' should not be adopted (or 'Court of Audit'; but not 'Court of Auditors', which is the official English title of a similar European Community institution). The Audit Court has seven divisions; appeal on points of law (*cassation*) lies to the Conseil d'État.

The last specialised court to be mentioned is likewise a national one and again has no counterpart in the English system: the *Cour de discipline budgétaire et financière*. This court exists to punish by way of fines any irregularities committed by public officials responsible for implementing State and local-authority budgets. That jurisdiction does not extend to ministers or local elected representatives such as mayors, but it does include a power to fine any public servant held responsible for delaying or preventing the execution of a monetary judgment of the Conseil d'État against a public authority. Cases may be referred to the court by the Speakers of the two Houses of Parliament, members of the government, the Audit Court and the regional audit boards. In the nature of things, the court's work is very limited and does not require a full-time court. The court has no permanent staff of its own and only six members, appointed for five years at a time: three from the Audit Court (including that court's President, who presides) and three from the Conseil d'État. As with the Audit Court, appeal on points of law lies to the Conseil d'État. Given the lack of any remotely similar institution in Britain, the court's title is not readily translatable and one probably cannot do better than the more or less word-for-word rendering 'Budget and Finance Disciplinary Court'.

Finally in this section, a brief mention should be made of the *Médiateur*. This office was established by an Act of 1973, amended in 1976. The word literally means 'mediator' – and the French title thus stresses the official's conciliatory rôle – but that sounds most improbable as the title of an official in English, and since the office broadly corresponds to that of the Parliamentary Commissioner for Administration in the United Kingdom (a title which, however, is too culture-specific to be acceptable as a translation), the best rendering is no doubt 'Ombudsman'. As in Britain, the Ombudsman in France investigates cases of maladministration, and complainants have to approach him through a member of Parliament (from either House in France) – though parliamentarians can also raise matters with him of their own motion. He is not himself a parliamentary official, however, and is appointed for a non-renewable term of only six years. Although the annual number of complaints he has received since 1977 has not been less than 4,000 and in some years has reached nearly 7,000, his arrival on the scene does not appear to have resulted in any reduction in the number of cases brought in the administrative courts.

6.7 Appellate administrative courts

Until 1989 appeal from the administrative courts (by way of *appel*) and from the specialised tribunals (nearly all by way of *cassation*[40]) lay solely to the Conseil d'État. One result of this was that by 1988 the Conseil, which was then hearing 7,000 to 8,000 cases a year,[41] had a backlog of over 25,000 cases. It was clear that something radical again had to be done to relieve the pressure (although it may be pointed out in passing that the Court of Cassation had a backlog of over 31,000 cases by then). This time it was impossible to shift any more of the Conseil d'État's burden onto the administrative courts of first instance, since they too were by now overstretched.[42] The solution found – and embodied in an Act of 31 December 1987, which came into force in January 1989 – was accordingly to model the hierarchy of administrative courts on that of the ordinary courts by creating an intermediate level of appellate jurisdiction: the *cour administrative d'appel* ('Administrative Court of Appeal').

40. The fact that the remedy of cassation is available from the Conseil d'État as well as the Court of Cassation is another reason for not in general translating *pourvoi en cassation* as an 'application to the Court of Cassation'.

41. In 1987 it tried 7,984 cases according to J. Massot and J. Marimbert's *Le Conseil d'État*, Notes et Études documentaires 4869–70 (La Documentation française, 1988), p. 251, or 6,938 cases according to the Ministry of Justice's *Annuaire statistique de la justice 1987* (La Documentation française, 1989), p. 43.

42. By the end of 1987 the thirty-three courts (including the seven overseas) had a backlog of over 100,000 cases between them.

This new jurisdiction is a major regional one, only five such courts having been established – at Paris, Bordeaux, Lyon, Nantes and Nancy.[43] These courts will initially hear appeals (by way of *appel*) from the courts of first instance in all actions for damages and in applications for judicial review other than those relating to regulations; their jurisdiction will steadily be enlarged over the next few years. Appeal lies from them to the Conseil d'État by way of *cassation* only. The Conseil d'État thus loses the greater part of its jurisdiction to hear full appeals (*appels*), while simultaneously having its cassation jurisdiction expanded.

The administrative courts of appeal of Paris and Lyon are both subdivided into three divisions, and the other three courts into two divisions. Each court is presided over by a member of the Conseil d'État transferred from his existing duties as such or else newly appointed for the purpose. The other judges have been drawn from a variety of sources and backgrounds, judicial and administrative. Cases are normally heard by a court of five judges if the court sits as a divisional court or of seven if it sits as a full court.

From these courts, then, appeal lies in the form of a *recours en cassation* (occasionally called *pourvoi en cassation*) ('appeal on points of law') to the Conseil d'État, and it is this august body which will now be described, with special reference to its judicial functions.

The Conseil d'État is an advisory as well as a judicial body, consisting of four *sections administratives* (covering different areas of policy), a *section du contentieux* and a *section du rapport et des études*. The word *section* here would normally be translated as 'section' (especially as other courts have *chambres*, which, it has been suggested above, should generally be rendered as 'divisions'). But 'section' is wholly unfamiliar in English as a term for a subdivision of a court, and this coupled with the fact that the *section du contentieux* is itself divided into ten *sous-sections* (which really can only be translated as 'sections', since 'subsection' not only sounds wrong but is familiar as a subdivision of an Act) tips the balance in favour of translating *section* as 'division'. The divisions of the Conseil d'État can therefore be referred to in English as 'the administrative divisions' and 'the Judicial Division' (the latter a translation which places the emphasis correctly on the particular function of the Division in contrast with the administrative functions of the other divisions, whereas the other possible translation commonly met with – 'Litigation Division' – perhaps focuses attention rather on the parties to, or the subject of, the dispute

43. Compare the figure of 30 ordinary courts of appeal.

brought before the court; and cf. the title 'Judicial Committee of the Privy Council' in Britain).

Contrary to what this pattern of organisation might initially suggest, about two-thirds – over a hundred – of the full-time working members of the Conseil d'État specialise in adjudication in the Judicial Division, so that although at least a third of the Conseil's work is advisory, it is increasingly overshadowed by its judicial function. Furthermore, with only a few exceptions, all members of the Conseil have to undertake both judicial and advisory duties, being simultaneously assigned to an administrative division and the Judicial Division.

The nominal President of the Conseil d'État is the Prime Minister, who, on the rare occasions when his right to preside is invoked, is represented by the Minister of Justice; in practice the Vice-President presides (cf. the Vice-Chancellor in the Chancery Division of the English High Court).

The senior members of the Conseil d'État are the *conseillers (d'État)*.[44] The term *conseiller* as a general title has already been mentioned (on p. 71 above). In this instance of its use to denote a specific rank of membership of the Conseil d'État, however, it cannot be translated merely as 'judge (of the Conseil d'État)' – and in any case, as has just been pointed out, the work of the Conseil is not only judicial; accordingly, the term can only be rendered as '(senior) member of the Conseil d'État' or else transcribed (for example when it follows a person's name to indicate his position).

The middle-ranking members of the Conseil are the *maîtres des requêtes* and the junior members are the *auditeurs*[45] (who may be *de première classe* or *de seconde classe*). There would seem to be two possible ways of coping with the translation of these terms: either to refer to both ranks collectively as 'junior members of the Conseil d'État' or, in cases where only the one rank or the other is mentioned, to adopt the translations suggested by Bridge – 'Legal Adviser' and 'Legal Assistant' for *maître des requêtes* and *auditeur* respectively. The latter course has the advantage of suggesting a hierarchical distinction such as in fact exists. An alternative, seeing that *maître des requêtes*, unlike *auditeurs*, lends itself to formally

44. In addition to the hundred or so *conseillers* who are permanent (*en service ordinaire*) there are approximately a dozen on secondment (*en service extraordinaire*) for four years at a time – civil servants from other departments of State, distinguished lawyers, trade-union leaders, etc. None of these, however, is assigned to the Judicial Division.

45. Also the title of the junior members of the Audit Court (see pp. 89–90 above).

equivalent translation, would be to translate that term as 'Master of Requests' (historically a not wholly unrelated office in the English legal system) and then translate *auditeur* as 'Legal Assistant' as before. If necessary, the *auditeurs de première classe* and the *auditeurs de seconde classe* can be distinguished as 'Legal Assistant Grade I' and 'Legal Assistant Grade II'. In the Judicial Division the *conseillers* actually decide the cases, while *maîtres des requêtes* take routine decisions, act as *commissaires du gouvernement* (see p. 113 below) and, like the *auditeurs*, act as *rapporteurs* ('rapporteurs' or 'reporting judges') – preparing cases for trial (the proceedings are in practice entirely in written form, notwithstanding a brief public hearing).[46]

The rôle of the administrative divisions of the Conseil d'État is to give the government confidential advisory opinions on proposed legislation, the appropriate division (or divisions jointly) revising bills and draft decrees, etc., in conjunction with the relevant ministry. (This process does not preclude a regulation's later being challenged as invalid in the administrative courts or before the Judicial Division of the Conseil, as the case may be.) More generally the Conseil acts as legal adviser to the government and to individual ministers. After examination by the appropriate division or divisions, the more important categories of enactment are reconsidered by the *assemblée générale ordinaire* ('the ordinary General Assembly', consisting of the Vice-President as chairman, the presidents of the six divisions, thirteen *conseillers* from the Judicial Division and three *conseillers* from each of the other divisions) or, rarely,[47] by the *assemblée générale plénière* ('the full General Assembly', consisting of the Vice-President as chairman, the presidents of the six divisions and all the *conseillers* – up to a hundred people).

The foregoing procedure is fairly lengthy, and in 1945 a *Commission permanente* ('Standing Committee') was established in order to provide a speedier alternative for urgent matters, the urgency of the bill, etc., to be certified by the Prime Minister. The committee consists of ten *conseillers* appointed for a year at a time and chaired by one of the division presidents, in practice the President of the Finance Division.

The majority of cases tried by the Judicial Division are heard by an odd number of judges (between five and nine of them) from two different sections sitting together, including the presidents and usually

46. In the administrative divisions, senior members as well as junior members are called upon to serve as *rapporteurs*.

47. Except in the period from mid-July to the beginning of September, when annual holidays make it impossible to convene any but a full General Assembly (paradoxical though this may sound).

also the other two *conseillers* of each section, a representative from one of the administrative divisions and the rapporteur for the case; one of the three deputy presidents (*présidents adjoints*) of the Division – or else the President himself (or occasionally even the Vice-President of the Conseil) – presides. This constitution of the court is known as *les sous-sections réunies* ('combined sections').

Since 1980 it has again been possible for the less important and less difficult cases to be heard by a single section, and in 1987 some 40 per cent of the cases heard by more than one judge were disposed of in this way. Since 1984 the presidents of the sections of the Judicial Division have likewise been empowered to determine certain straightforward cases sitting alone, mostly those in which the decision is largely a formality.

Cases which present greater difficulty are heard by the Judicial Division sitting as a divisional court and comprising a maximum of seventeen judges: the President, the three deputy presidents, the ten section presidents, two *conseillers* from the administrative divisions and the rapporteur. An odd number must sit, and the quorum is nine. In 1987 the Division sitting as such heard 47 cases.

The hardest cases of all – and especially those which are likely to have major political or administrative repercussions – are reserved for the *assemblée du contentieux*, which is composed of the Vice-President of the Conseil (who presides and has a casting vote), the presidents of all the divisions, the three deputy presidents of the Judicial Division and the president and rapporteur of the section which initially considered the case. The *assemblée* heard only 14 cases in 1987. *Assemblée du contentieux* is not easy to translate. 'Full court' is not quite specific enough – and has already been used for the *assemblée plénière* of the Court of Cassation. The best rendering is probably simply 'Judicial Assembly'.

In addition to hearing appeals on points of law from subordinate courts and tribunals the Conseil also retains some original jurisdiction, as was pointed out on p. 88 above. Furthermore, the 1987 Act referred to at the beginning of this section introduced three other important changes apart from those already mentioned.

Firstly, appeals to the Conseil on points of law are now subject to that court's leave, granted or withheld in a judgment given by a three-member *Commission d'admission des pourvois en cassation* – perhaps best translated simply as 'Appeal Committee' (as in the House of Lords) or else as 'Leave Committee', since anything longer would seem unduly cumbrous as a title in English.

Secondly, whereas previously the Conseil, on quashing a judgment, would, like the Court of Cassation, remit the case to another court or tribunal of the same category as the one whose judgment had been set aside (assuming there to be more than one such – otherwise to the original court or tribunal), which then had to apply the Conseil's view of the law to the facts (of which it remained the sole judge), the Conseil now has power to quash without remitting and to determine the merits itself where the interests of proper administration of justice so require – and is obliged to do so where one and the same case has been appealed to the Conseil twice in succession.

Thirdly, before deciding a case before them the administrative courts of first instance and of appeal may now – at their discretion, but no appeal lies against the decision – refer difficult new legal issues arising in a large number of cases to the Conseil d'État for an opinion (*avis*). Theoretically the Conseil's opinion, which has to be given within three months, is not binding, but it is unlikely to be ignored by the court which has taken the initiative of seeking it. Within the existing French system this new, optional procedure is reminiscent of the *recours en appréciation de légalité* ('application for review of legality') which has to be made to an administrative court for a ruling on a preliminary issue (*question préjudicielle*) when in a civil case[48] a defendant raises a plea of illegality (*exception d'illégalité*) claiming that an administrative act being relied on against him is unlawful. Within the English system the new French procedure is comparable only to an appeal by way of case stated, but in that procedure the High Court's ruling on the law may be sought as of right and the lower court is bound by that ruling; the French procedure is perhaps rather more similar to a reference of an issue of Community law to the European Court of Justice in Luxembourg under Article 177 of the Treaty of Rome (although in that instance too the European Court's view of the relevant Community law is binding on the national court).

Finally, before this account of the Conseil d'État is concluded, mention must be made of the remaining division, the *section du rapport et des études* ('Report and Research Division'). The rôle of this division has expanded ever since its creation in 1963 as a Report Committee. It has three main tasks. Firstly, it is responsible, with the assistance of all the other divisions, for producing detailed statistics and an annual report on the Conseil's activities. Secondly, at the request of the Prime Minister or on the initiative of the Conseil's Vice-President,[49] it draws up studies of current adminis-

48. But not in a criminal case – see p. 69 above.

49. Who may himself have been asked for such a study by the Ombudsman.

trative and legal problems for the government's attention; these will usually contain suggestions for reform. Thirdly, it is responsible for monitoring the execution of the Conseil's judgments, for which purpose it has available to it, if needed, a number of conciliatory procedures and, since 1980, some rather more coercive measures. The Division also coordinates the relations of the Conseil and its members with foreign courts and international bodies.

6.8 The *Tribunal des conflits*

There remain to be discussed two judicial bodies which are of the highest rank but lie outside and above the hierarchies of the ordinary and the administrative courts.

The dual system of courts, reflecting and reinforcing the separation of administrative from judicial functions, is not wholly without drawbacks. In particular, it is sometimes uncertain – but always of crucial importance – whether a given action should be brought in the ordinary courts or in the administrative ones.[50] Such a case might, for example, be one where a tort has been committed by a public servant and the question arises whether he was acting in a private or in his official capacity. To resolve such matters of doubt, there has existed since 1872 the *Tribunal des conflits*, a title which seems best translated as 'Jurisdiction Disputes Court'. It consists of three *conseillers en service ordinaire* elected by and from the Conseil d'État and three *conseillers* elected by and from the Court of Cassation; these in turn, together with the Minister of Justice, who is the President of the Court, elect two further judges – in practice one each from the Conseil d'État and the Court of Cassation – and all nine then elect two substitutes, again one each from the two supreme courts. The judges hold office for three years. The Minister of Justice in practice sits – other than for the election of new judges – only on the extremely rare occasions when his casting vote is needed, and his place is taken by a vice-president elected by the

50. A similar problem used to arise in the English courts before the fusion of the courts of common law and the courts of equity in the Supreme Court of Judicature in 1873–5. The present division of labour between the three main divisions of the English High Court, all of which theoretically retain full jurisdiction to try any matter, is by comparison one largely of administrative convenience in the interests of efficiency, although (as pointed out in note 5 of Chapter 4 on p. 47 above) recent decisions of the House of Lords have established the principle that actions to assert public-law rights against public administrative bodies must be brought by way of an application to the Queen's Bench Divisional Court for judicial review and not by means of an ordinary action.

court for three years from its own midst, the post going to a member of the Conseil d'État and a member of the Court of Cassation alternately.

Conflicts of jurisdiction may arise in three ways. Firstly, when a private citizen sues a public servant in the ordinary courts, the administrative authorities may wish to argue that the matter falls to be decided by the administrative courts under public law. In this event, known as *conflit positif (d'attribution(s))*, the local prefect will *élever le conflit* ('raise the question of jurisdiction') by entering a *déclinatoire de compétence* ('plea in bar alleging want of jurisdiction' or, more succinctly, 'plea of no jurisdiction'), in which he will argue that the ordinary court in question has no jurisdiction to hear the case. (He is not estopped from doing this for the first time on bringing an appeal, but the plea cannot be raised in the Court of Cassation.) If the court rejects the plea, the prefect can apply to the Jurisdiction Disputes Court for a final ruling, which must be given within three months. If the original court accepts the plea, the plaintiff must either sue in the administrative courts or else appeal to a higher ordinary court.

A second type of conflict, known as a *conflit négatif (d'attribution(s))*, has all but been eliminated since 1960. It arose where a court against whose decision no form of appeal lay – in practice the Court of Cassation or the Conseil d'État – had disclaimed jurisdiction in a case and a court of the other hierarchy, duly seised of the case, disagreed and also disclaimed jurisdiction. In such an event, it was left to the parties to apply to the Jurisdiction Disputes Court. Since 1960, however, the second court disclaiming jurisdiction has itself been obliged to refer such a case to the Jurisdiction Disputes Court, and it has also been possible to prevent a conflict arising in the first place: the court originally seised (the Court of Cassation or the Conseil d'État) may of its own motion refer any case raising serious difficulties or important questions of jurisdiction to the Jurisdiction Disputes Court direct for a binding decision before ever the matter is brought before any court of the other hierarchy.

Finally, in a third – very rare – case of conflict, known as *conflit/contrariété de jugements* or *conflit de décisions*, where either an ordinary court or an administrative court may have jurisdiction (depending on who is being sued as defendant) but have both declined to grant relief after reaching conflicting decisions on the facts (to take a celebrated example,[51] whether a road accident was in

51. Which could no longer arise today, the ordinary courts having been given jurisdiction by statute to try road-accident cases even where they involve a public-service vehicle, as was noted in Section 6.2.

fact caused by a private citizen or by a public servant in the course of his duties), the plaintiff himself can apply to the Jurisdiction Disputes Court for a ruling; and in such circumstances (only), that court will itself decide the merits of the case instead of merely ruling on the jurisdictional issue and assigning the case to one or the other hierarchy of courts.

In all, the Jurisdiction Disputes Court currently hears between thirty and seventy cases a year.

The terms *conflit/contrariété de jugements* and *conflit de décisions* can all be satisfactorily rendered in English as 'conflicting judgments' or 'conflicting decisions'. But the only possible translations of *conflit positif* and *conflit negatif* – 'positive conflict' and 'negative conflict' – are so unclear in meaning in English that some explanation, probably going rather beyond a mere gloss, is necessary.

Before we leave the subject of jurisdictional conflict, it is perhaps worth pointing out that conflicts of jurisdiction between the civil and the criminal ordinary courts are decided by the Court of Cassation.

6.9 The *Conseil constitutionnel*

The *Conseil constitutionnel*, which was created by the 1958 Constitution, is the nearest thing to a constitutional court that France possesses, but its powers are much more restricted than those of, say, the United States Supreme Court or the German Federal Constitutional Court in constitutional matters: indeed, it is a *juridiction d'attribution*, having no general or inherent jurisdiction. In addition to all past presidents of the Republic, who are entitled to sit as of right, the *Conseil constitutionnel* has nine members (usually but not necessarily lawyers), all appointed for a non-renewable nine-year term – three of them by the President of the Republic (who also decides which member shall preside), three by the Speaker of the Senate and three by the Speaker of the National Assembly. Each nominating authority appoints a new judge every three years.

The *Conseil* has essentially a dual – adjudicative and advisory – function, which it exercises in several different fields. Firstly, all institutional Acts (*lois organiques* – see p. 62 above) have to be submitted to it before they are promulgated for confirmation that they conform to the Constitution. Other statutes and international treaties are scrutinised by the *Conseil* only at the specific request – again before promulgation – of either the President of the Republic, the Speaker of the Senate, the Speaker of the National Assembly or (since 1974) sixty senators or sixty MPs (*députés*). In either case the *Conseil*'s ruling as to constitutionality or unconstitutionality has to be given within a month – or within a week if the government asks for urgent consideration – and is binding, so that the legal instrument under consideration (or the relevant part(s) of it) cannot be promulgated or ratified, as the case may be, until any amendments indicated in the ruling are made (or the Constitution is amended).

More generally, the *Conseil* is responsible for ensuring that Parliament and the government both keep within their respective legislative spheres as laid down in Articles 34 and 37 of the Constitution (see Section 5.2). Thus, where the government wishes to amend by decree an existing statute passed by Parliament after 1958, the Prime Minister must refer the Act in question to the *Conseil* for determination of whether the subject-matter properly falls within the legislative sphere of Parliament or within that of the executive. Similarly, it is open to the government to challenge Parliament's right to legislate on a given matter; if there is disagreement between the government and Parliament on the point in respect of proposed legislation, the government or the Speaker of the relevant House can refer the matter to the *Conseil* for a ruling, which must be given within a week.

While the *Conseil constitutionnel* is the only body competent to declare an Act of Parliament unconstitutional, it cannot do so once an Act has been promulgated; nor can it review at all the constitutionality of regulations, whose legality can only be challenged in the administrative courts. Given, too, that its primary function under the Constitution is to ensure that Parliament does not exceed its constitutional powers, it has also disclaimed any jurisdiction over statutes approved by national referendum.

In addition to these constitutional functions in relation to legislation, the *Conseil constitutionnel* also adjudicates on the validity of referendums and presidential and parliamentary elections in cases of dispute and has a supervisory and advisory rôle in respect of the organisation of them.[52] Finally, the *Conseil* is the only body authorised to rule on whether or not the President of the Republic is temporarily or permanently unable to perform the duties of his office (e.g. for health reasons) or whether the presidency has become vacant for any other reason (e.g. the resignation or death of the incumbent); and it must be consulted before any exercise by the President of his emergency powers under Article 16 of the Consti-

52. Local elections, however, come under the jurisdiction of the Conseil d'État.

tution. In all, the *Conseil* hands down roughly two dozen decisions a year, a figure which rises to about 70 in parliamentary-election years.

Although the *Conseil* appears to have only a circumscribed rôle (owing mainly to the very small class of persons who, in constitutional matters, can seek a ruling from it), it has proved remarkably active in the constitutional field since the early 1970s, largely thanks to the 1974 reform which conferred the right to apply to it on parliamentarians (sixty senators or sixty MPs), a right which has been amply exercised. For the present, however, the *Conseil* cannot be described as a true supreme constitutional court, since it is not a supreme appellate court like the United States Supreme Court (although its rulings are binding on the Court of Cassation and the Conseil d'État) nor, like that court or the constitutional courts of Germany and Italy, can it rule on the constitutionality of legislation once promulgated. The question thus arises, to what extent it is really a court at all. If the reasoning adduced above when the translation of *Conseil d'État* was being considered is applied in the case of the *Conseil constitutionnel*, the word-for-word translation 'Constitutional Council' would have to be rejected in favour of 'Constitutional Court'. But it is arguable that, since the body barely qualifies as a court, 'Constitutional Council' would not be misleading and is in fact probably the more accurate translation of the two.

–7–

The legal professions

7.1 *Auxiliaires de justice*

In terms of the English legal system, 'the legal profession' is usually understood to comprise the separate careers of barrister and solicitor. In France, according to René David,[1] there is no general concept of a legal profession: anybody can call himself a lawyer and practise as such as long as he does not infringe the monopoly granted by statute to certain lawyers for certain purposes (e.g. pleading in court) or usurp a title (such as *notaire*) to which he has no right. In England 'consulting one's lawyer' would invariably mean consulting one's solicitor; in France it would generally be taken to mean consulting one's *avocat*. For the purposes of this chapter, 'legal professions' should be understood in a very broad sense as covering all and any of the different rôles in the French legal system, for most – though not all – of which the practitioner has to be qualified as a lawyer. In French the persons to be discussed here are all designated generically as *auxiliaires de (la) justice*, a term defined in Guillien and Vincent's *Lexique de termes juridiques* as 'hommes de loi dont la mission est destinée à faciliter la marche de l'instance et la bonne administration de la justice'. This designation might perhaps be translated as 'officers of the court',[2] or else as 'court auxiliaries'.

In France the division of labour corresponding to that between barrister and solicitor in England is only approximately that between *avocat* and *notaire*, who are the kinds of lawyer with whom the public most commonly comes into direct contact. The reason why the correspondence is only roughly similar is that while a *notaire*'s work would in England be done very largely by a solicitor, the latter's functions are potentially – and usually in practice – much

1. R. David, *English Law and French Law* (Stevens & Sons and Eastern Law House, 1980), p. 49.
2. Cf. English solicitors, who are officers of the Supreme Court.

wider than those of a *notaire* and would in France be split between an *avocat*, a *notaire* and a *conseil juridique*.

In Scotland the practitioner corresponding broadly to *avocat* is officially (and in England is in some literary and other non-technical contexts[3]) called an 'advocate', a word obviously cognate with *avocat*. In England the professional equivalent would be 'barrister', a lawyer whose work is much the same as – though slightly less wide-ranging than – that of the French *avocat*. Whereas in England barristers can be approached by clients (other than representatives of one or two specified professions) only through a solicitor, however, in France the *avocat* is consulted direct. This makes it practicable for him to provide, as he does, some of the services that in England would be provided by a solicitor, and there are more than three times as many *avocats* in France as there are barristers in England. Conversely, *avocats* cannot remain members of the bar if they take salaried employment, for example as a company's in-house lawyer. These differences are not such as to preclude the translation 'barrister', however. At the same time, though, it should be noted that, just as many international organisations have official titles in more than one language, so European Community barristers, who are now allowed to practise in any member State, must use only their original official title (e.g. *avocat*, *Rechtsanwalt*, 'barrister'), not a translation; and this is the practice followed in the English-language versions of the judgments of the Court of Justice of the European Communities in Luxembourg and of the European Court of Human Rights in Strasbourg wherever either the title of a particular named individual or else a specific national profession is concerned. In a court context, *avocat* (*de la défense*) will often be translated as 'counsel (for the defence)' (who may also be referred to in French as the *défenseur* – not to be confused with *défendeur*, the defendant or respondent in a civil lawsuit).[4]

French barristers give legal advice and can plead in any court in the land (except the Court of Cassation, the Conseil d'État, the

3. E.g. 'He was one of the greatest advocates of his day.'

4. Other ways of dealing with this term will be appropriate in different contexts. Thus, where an *avocat* is performing a service that in England would or might be provided by a solicitor, or in a text (e.g. a Community directive) applying to both barristers and solicitors in England (but only to *avocats* in France), the generic term 'lawyer' may be used as a substitute in an English version, though obviously this is not a translation in the strict sense. Similarly, as hinted in the first paragraph of this chapter, in the utterance 'Il faut que je consulte mon avocat' the term should be rendered as 'lawyer' or, more accurately still, 'solicitor', both of which *are* genuine context-determined translations (functional equivalents).

Audit Court and the Jurisdiction Disputes Court – see below), though in practice the formal procedural work is always done by a local barrister. Until 1972 all the written work in civil cases was done by an *avoué*,[5] who was the litigant's official (and, unlike the *avocat*, compulsory) legal representative and, as such, represented his client in all the formal procedural steps of a case. In this work *avoués* and *agréés* resembled solicitors rather than barristers but were in fact midway between the two, and the terms – now rarely met with – are accordingly best transcribed and glossed.[6] Since September 1972, however, the professions of *avocat* and *avoué* have been largely merged, with the result that ordinary *avocats* now do all the work before the lower courts, while *avoués* have survived only in proceedings in the courts of appeal (*avoués près la cour d'appel*) and *agréés* no longer exist, having become *avocats*.

In the Court of Cassation and the Conseil d'État litigants are represented for all purposes by one of about ninety special *avocats aux conseils*, i.e. *avocats à la Cour de cassation* ('barristers at the Court of Cassation'), who are at the same time *avocats au Conseil d'État* ('barristers at the Conseil d'État'); they form a separate bar and have a monopoly of representation not only before the Court of Cassation and the Conseil d'État but also before the Jurisdiction Disputes Court and the Audit Court (and they can also appear in other courts).

All other barristers have to be members of the bar attached to their local Tribunal de Grande Instance, known as the *ordre des avocats* or *barreau* (both corresponding broadly to 'bar') of the given town or city. Each bar elects from among its own members a *conseil de l'ordre* ('bar council') – which has administrative and disciplinary functions – and a *bâtonnier* ('chairman of the bar'), who presides over both the bar as a whole and its council. The profession is a graduate one: all entrants must have at least a Master's degree in law and have gained admission to and successfully completed a year's professional training course leading to the *certificat d'aptitude à la profession d'avocat* ('Qualifying Certificate for the Bar', 'Bar Certificate'). Such candidates will be admitted as trainee barristers for a two-year period, upon completion of which they will be entered on the bar roll (*inscrits au tableau*). Lastly, while they may

5. In the commercial courts, by an *agréé*, who, however, combined the functions of an *avoué* and an *avocat*.

6. In Mauritius, *avoués* (who have survived as a distinct profession) are known in English as 'attorneys' (who once formed a similar separate profession in England). This indeed seems the only possible translation, so long as no confusion with the different, American attorneys is possible in a given context.

enter into partnership with colleagues, *avocats* (unlike barristers – or solicitors – in England) are not allowed to take any salaried employment except as assistants of other *avocats* or as university law lecturers, though this position may soon change.

The other main legal profession – an ancient one – is that of the *notaire*, who holds an important position. In England his work would be done mainly by a solicitor but partly also by the Chancery bar and by a notary. *Notaires* have a virtual monopoly of practice in conveyancing and matters concerning marriage settlements and succession. Like English solicitors they are often the confidential advisers of families and businesses, in which capacity they enjoy even higher prestige as, unlike solicitors, their numbers are limited by law; whereas in England and Wales there were at least 50,000 solicitors by 1989, there were only some 7,300 or so *notaires* in France – a figure not greatly in excess of the number of barristers in England. The standard comparative account of the work of a *notaire* is still Brown's 1953 article 'The office of the notary in France', which is worth quoting:

> The functions, which in England have accrued to the solicitor, in France have passed to the notary, so that except for the absence of litigation, his daily work is remarkably like that of the solicitor. There is, as it were, a common territory in which both operate, and on either side a domain special to each – the solicitor has his litigation and the notary his authenticity [i.e. the drawing up of authoritative formal documents]. But the solicitor may also poach in the notary's preserve in the guise of a notary public.[7]

Thus, while the common translation 'notary' – used by Brown – is obviously the *formal* equivalent of *notaire* (and, alas, so many translators – and not just amateur ones – allow themselves to be mesmerised by formal correspondence), it is equally clearly not remotely equivalent functionally and must usually be rejected (unless qualified as 'French notary'). The closest equivalent in English is plainly 'solicitor' (this is indeed an excellent example of how a functional translation must take precedence over even an exact formal equivalent which does not correspond functionally[8]); but there are three caveats. Firstly, it will in some linguistic con-

7. L. N. Brown, 'The office of the notary in France', *International and Comparative Law Quarterly*, 2 (1953), 60–71 (p. 71).

8. As a solicitor's work is usually much wider in range than a *notaire*'s, combining as it does parts of the work of a *notaire*, an *avocat* and a *conseil juridique*, it would of course be wholly inaccurate to translate 'solicitor' as *notaire* in French, however.

texts be possible and advisable to specify 'French solicitor', though that would be unnecessary in, say, a French novel – such as Duhamel's *Le Notaire du Havre*. Secondly, and more importantly, while most of the work done by a *notaire* in France is done by a solicitor in England (so that 'Il faut que je consulte mon notaire' would, like 'Il faut que je consulte mon avocat' noted above, usually be translated correctly in English as 'I must see my solicitor'), there will be circumstances in which the service performed by the *notaire* (in particular, the authentication of documents) would likewise be done by a notary public in England – in which case 'notary' *would* be the proper translation. Finally, just as the French term *avocat* is sometimes transcribed in an English translation, so it will be appropriate in certain contexts (e.g. when referring to a named individual or to the specific French profession) to employ the French term *notaire* in a translation.

The corporate organisation of the profession is fairly complex and it is unnecessary to describe it here. The profession is essentially a graduate one, like that of *avocat*, it being normally necessary to have a Master's degree in law and to have completed three years' professional training and passed a qualifying examination. Again like *avocats*, *notaires* may work in partnership, but no form of salaried employment is permissible. As *notaires* hold public office (they are *officiers publics et ministériels* – see below), they are also required to live in the locality specified in their warrant of appointment.

A third major legal profession is that of *conseil juridique* ('legal adviser', 'legal consultant'[9]). These are professional lawyers not qualified to call themselves *avocats*, *avoués* or *notaires* and whose work consists mainly in giving legal advice and drawing up deeds. Such legal advisers may also assist and represent clients *vis-à-vis* administrative authorities and even in the commercial courts and, for certain matters, in district courts, hence their categorisation as officers of the court. Some advisers may specialise in tax affairs, in which case they call themselves *conseils fiscaux* ('tax advisers', 'tax consultants').

Before 1972 the profession was wholly unregulated, but the 1971 Act which reformed certain legal professions introduced compulsory registration as qualified (graduate) lawyers with the local *procureur de la République* (see Section 7.2), who is responsible for supervision of the profession. Legal advisers may establish them-

9. René David's translation 'legal counsel' (*English Law and French Law*, p. 54) is likely to cause confusion with 'counsel' used in the usual sense of 'barrister'.

selves anywhere in the country; like ordinary *avocats*, they are private practitioners but may combine in partnerships; they may not take salaried employment except as assistants of other legal advisers. There are currently some 4,800 of them.

Two other officers of the court should be briefly mentioned. Nearly all the ordinary and administrative courts described in Chapter 6 have a *secrétariat-greffe* – a body of administrative staff headed by a *greffier en chef* assisted by *greffiers*. *Greffiers* are technically members of the courts they serve, but although they must be present in order to assist the judges at court hearings, they do not themselves exercise any judicial power and are civil servants. Apart from their general administrative duties, they are responsible for preparing transcripts of court hearings, drawing up and distributing judgments, keeping the court register and acting as custodians and archivists of all court documents. In the administrative courts they are also responsible for service of process. There is not really any equivalent office in the English legal system, and the usual translation 'registrar' is somewhat inaccurate in view of the fact that a *greffier* has no judicial functions. 'Clerk of the court' would probably be a more exact rendering, as suggested by Harrap's dictionary; but since *secrétariat-greffe* (commonly abbreviated to *greffe*, which is the official title in the case of the commercial courts) can really only be translated as 'registry', thc balance is tipped in favour of retaining the usual translation 'registrar' for *greffier (en chef)* and, if the distinction is needed, 'assistant registrar' for *greffier*.

Finally, *huissiers (de justice)* act either as court bailiffs (responsible for enforcement of judgments, collection of debts and, in the ordinary courts, service of process[10]) or else principally as ushers during court sittings (*huissiers audienciers*), thus combining in one office what in England are two quite separate functions. In country areas, more particularly, *huissiers* can also undertake administrative tasks such as property management. The common translation 'bailiff' (or 'sheriff's officer') is therefore not wholly adequate, especially as bailiffs are strictly officers of the county courts in England, whereas the sheriff is the enforcement officer only for the High Court. The only reasonably accurate translation is O'Rooney's 'court usher and bailiff', though *either* 'court usher' *or* 'bailiff' will usually suffice when the text is clearly referring to only the one

10. On the instructions of the court or if retained by a private citizen, they also make *constats* – official reports on factual situations (e.g. road accidents or adultery), including inventories of premises, etc.

function or the other.

Now that the professions of the main officers of the court have been described, two further classificatory terms must be introduced: *officier public* and, more restricted in meaning, *officier ministériel*.

Officiers publics ('public (legal) officers') are those whose witnessing of proceedings or issuing or signing of documents, by virtue of their office, confers authority (i.e. official character) on them.[11] Such officers include *notaires*, *greffiers*, *huissiers* and also mayors (who officiate at weddings and are responsible for the registration of births, marriages and deaths).

Of those, *notaires*, the *greffiers* of the commercial courts[12] and *huissiers* are additionally *officiers ministériels*, as are also *avoués* and the barristers who practise at the Court of Cassation and the Conseil d'État (but not other barristers). *Officiers ministériels* enjoy a monopoly in their spheres of activity and are appointed for life by the State in the person of the Minister of Justice, though they are not thereafter directly answerable to the Minister or his subordinates. Upon retirement they have the right (*droit de présentation*) to propose a succcssor, to whom, if approved, they will sell their *office* (more commonly called *charge*, both terms being best translated as 'practice').[13] With the exception of the barristers practising at the Court of Cassation and the Conseil d'État, who negotiate fees with their clients like ordinary barristers, *officiers ministériels* are remunerated by the State according to a fixed scale.

The term *officier ministériel* is difficult to translate. The adjective *ministériel* does not, of course, relate to a government ministry but to *ministère* in the older sense of 'duty' or 'function' (cf. *ministère public*, discussed in the next section, and *le ministère d'un avocat*). In English the sense of the cognate word 'ministerial' meaning 'concerned with the execution of orders or law' – indicated as being archaic in *The Concise Oxford Dictionary* but not so indicated in the article on 'ministerial functions' in Walker's *Oxford Companion to*

11. Documents so issued or signed become conclusive evidence of what they purport to attest unless challenged as forgeries by means of a court action known as *inscription de faux*.

12. Court registrars were all both public officers and *officiers ministériels* until 1967, but from the end of that year onwards, although remaining public officers, all except the registrars of the commercial courts were gradually made civil servants, a process completed by the end of 1977.

13. A single practice may be held by a partnership; thus, although (as stated on p. 104 above) there are some ninety *avocats aux conseils*, the number of practices is strictly limited to sixty.

Law – appears to correspond in meaning. In his article on the French notary, cited earlier in this section, Brown uses the term 'ministerial official'. Although accurate, that expression would nowadays be likely to be understood (if at all) as meaning an 'official from a ministry' and accordingly cannot be recommended unless its sense is very clear from the context (which is unlikely). At the same time, however, 'law official' and 'legal official' are both so unspecific as to be useless (and 'law officer' would again be misleading), so it seems that the French term must be transcribed and glossed.

7.2 *Magistrats*

Since one of the major differences between the English and French judicial systems lies in the method of training judges, something must be said in this chapter about the judiciary. Professional judges in France greatly exceed their English counterparts in number – there are perhaps three times as many of them – and are only exceptionally recruited from among senior barristers.

The judges of the non-specialised ordinary and administrative courts, including – since December 1958, when an ordinance abolished the office of *juge de paix* ('stipendiary magistrate') – the judges of the district courts, have all normally trained as judges and civil servants respectively from the outset.

The judges of the ordinary courts train for two years at the *École nationale de la magistrature* in Bordeaux, though over half of that time is spent attached to a court and a month is spent in Paris. Four additional months' in-service training must be undertaken during the first eight years of the judge's career. The title of the *École* is not easy to translate convincingly into English: perhaps 'National Legal Service College' comes nearest to sounding plausible, given that 'School' does not have the connotations of prestige (and of postgraduate study) that the word *École* has in French. (And cf. the British Civil Service College; the term *magistrature* will be discussed separately later in this section.) Selection for admission to the college as an *auditeur de justice* (as the students are known) is normally by means of one of two competitive examinations, one of which is open to graduates (not necessarily in law) and the other to certain civil servants. Entry confers a salary and the status of full member of the judiciary. An average of approximately 2,000 candidates currently apply each year, of whom about 14 per cent are accepted. At the end of his training the student is usually appointed to an ordinary court in the provinces – and as a judge is irremovable (*inamovible*)[14] – but may alternatively be appointed to the *ministère public* (see below) or to the Ministry of Justice.

The judges of the administrative courts, as civil servants, train – after selection by similar methods – at the *École nationale d'administration* ('National Civil Service College') like other civil servants, and the best graduates from the college who want to be judges usually choose to be assigned to the Conseil d'État or the Audit Court; others will go to the first-instance administrative courts (from whose senior members the judges of the administrative courts of appeal will largely be drawn after the initial transitional period during which special arrangements have been made for recruitment from other sources). In theory, as administrative judges are not *magistrats* in the narrow sense (see p. 71 above), they are not irremovable; but in practice their independence is no less than that of their colleagues in the ordinary courts.

The professional judges of the ordinary courts (*juges* and *conseillers*), who, as was pointed out earlier, are the only judges who belong to the judicial power (*autorité judiciaire*) in the French understanding of that concept, are known collectively as the *magistrature assise* (or *magistrature du siège*). A very widespread error of translation is to render *magistrature* as 'magistracy' – as in Amos and Walton's admittedly somewhat hesitant translation of *magistrature assise* as '"seated magistracy"' (if one may interpret the use of inverted commas as betokening some – legitimate! – misgivings). In so far as it is used at all, the term 'magistracy' (or 'magistrature') in modern English refers (in a legal context) solely to the office or function of a magistrate or to magistrates collectively. The expression *magistrature assise* can be rendered without difficulty as 'the judges of the ordinary courts' – or, if the context is clear enough, simply 'the judiciary' or 'the bench'.

The word *magistrature* is often used by itself to mean 'the judiciary', but other than in a very loose sense it is not true to say, as René David does on p. 50 of his *English Law and French Law*, that 'the French word *magistrat* means judge' (especially as the judges of the administrative courts are not strictly *magistrats*). This is because the terms *magistrature assise/du siège* coexist and contrast with *magistrature debout/du parquet*.

The *parquet*, as it is more commonly known, was for a long time one of the most distinctive French legal institutions of all (in the

14. But if appointed as a *juge d'instruction* (see Section 8.4), is removable from performing his duties in that capacity in a given case.

eyes of an English lawyer). Its formal name is the *ministère public*, and until very recently it had no equivalent in the English legal system, although in Scotland the Crown Office (consisting of the Lord Advocate, the Solicitor-General (for Scotland) and the Advocates-Depute and to which local procurators-fiscal are answerable) exercised, as it still does, similar functions in respect of public prosecution. The nearest existing institution in English law was the Office of the Director of Public Prosecutions, who is subject to the authority of the Attorney-General. The Director, however, while in theory able to take over the conduct of any prosecution at any stage, in practice acted in only a small number of serious cases, and the great majority of prosecutions were brought by the police or local authorities. But following the report of the Royal Commission on Criminal Procedure in 1981, a Crown Prosecution Service was set up in England and Wales and came fully into operation in October 1986. It is headed by the Director of Public Prosecutions and the prosecution of most criminal offences is now exclusively in its hands.

Ministère public and *parquet*, however, are not accurately rendered in English as, say, 'Public/State Prosecutor's Office', even though in texts concerned solely with criminal proceedings this (preferably, perhaps, without initial capital letters, as there are many such offices in France) will usually be an acceptable and indeed helpful translation.[15] The translation difficulty arises for two main reasons.

Firstly, the members of the *ministère public*, although responsible for the conduct of all criminal proceedings in respect of serious offences (*délits* and *crimes*[16]), also have an important rôle to play in civil proceedings, where they may intervene as what Kahn-Freund, Lévy and Rudden call 'as it were, institutionalised *amici curiae*',[17] representing the interests of the law, their view of which they present to the court, giving an objective appraisal in the light of the case-law and making submissions (*conclusions*) as to the course to be adopted by the court – submissions which may sometimes call for a change in the court's attitude as expressed in earlier cases. More accurately, perhaps, they represent the interest of society as perceived by the executive – whose agents they are, despite enjoying the status of *magistrat*. They also perform functions such as repre-

15. In texts describing court proceedings, *ministère public* can often be translated more briefly as 'the prosecution'.

16. See Section 8.1.

17. Sir Otto Kahn-Freund, C. Lévy and B. Rudden, *A Source-book on French Law*, 2nd edn (Clarendon Press, 1979), p. 286.

senting persons under a disability that in England would often be carried out by the Official Solicitor acting as next friend or as guardian *ad litem*. Additionally they direct the work of the police (criminal-investigation officers) and have supervisory powers or practical responsibilities in relation to *officiers publics*, *officiers ministériels*, the execution of ordinary-court judgments, the enforcement of sentences, criminal records, legal aid and registers of births, marriages and deaths, to name but the most important of their administrative duties.

Secondly, the *ministère public* is organised as a decentralised national hierarchy headed by the Minister of Justice, with subordinate officials of differing ranks attached to courts of different levels. Thus, immediately below the Minister and each answerable directly to him, *procureurs généraux* preside over the *parquets* attached to the Court of Cassation (where the *procureur général* is also competent for the High Court of Justice) and to each court of appeal; in the Court of Cassation the *procureur général*'s subordinates are the *avocats généraux* ('advocates-general'), led by the *premier avocat général* ('Principal Advocate-General'), while in the courts of appeal his subordinates are advocates-general and *substituts généraux*. At the Tribunal de Grande Instance the *ministère public* is headed by a *procureur de la République*, whose subordinates are one or more *procureurs adjoints* (in the largest courts only) and numbers of *premier substituts* (except in the smallest courts) and *substituts*. The *procureur de la République* also acts in certain cases in the district courts within the area of the Tribunal de Grande Instance to which he is attached, but for all save the most serious petty offences the *ministère public* is usually represented (in the police court) by a policeman of the rank of superintendent (*commissaire*) or his delegate, or occasionally by the local mayor. In the Assize Court it is the *procureur général* of the Court of Appeal who acts where the assizes are held in the town in which the Court of Appeal has its seat, otherwise the *procureur de la République*, who can, when needed, also appear in any other ordinary court of first instance.

All the foregoing officials can be described as *officiers du ministère public* (not to be confused with the *officiers ministériels* discussed in Section 7.1). Unlike the judges, none of them is irremovable, and while usually free to represent the public interest as they see fit, they are all required to carry out any instructions given them in any particular case by their superiors (or else to resign), subject only to the principle 'la plume est serve, mais la parole est libre' (or 'si la plume est serve, la parole est libre'), i.e. having made their formal written submissions to the court as instructed, they are at liberty to put the contrary case orally.

Among the administrative courts only the Audit Court has a *parquet* of similar status, headed by a *procureur général* whose subordinates are *avocats généraux* and who also acts in the Budget and Finance Disciplinary Court. In the other administrative courts (including the Conseil d'État) and the Jurisdiction Disputes Court a somewhat similar function is performed quite independently by *commissaires du gouvernement* ('Government Commissioners'). Most of these are not *magistrats* in the strict sense but – despite their name, which is a complete misnomer[18] – are members of the courts concerned who have been temporarily appointed to watch over and represent the interests of the law and do not speak for the government at all – indeed, they often recommend annulment of administrative measures. (It may be pointed out in passing that the six advocates-general at the Court of Justice of the European Communities play a comparable rôle.) The *commissaires du gouvernement* attached to the *chambres régionales des comptes*, however, are the subordinates of the *procureur général* at the Audit Court.

The institution of the *ministère public* having been described, how are the terms left untranslated in the foregoing paragraphs to be rendered in English? The most difficult to translate is undoubtedly *ministère public*. Assuming that the rendering 'Public Ministry' – whether offered in all seriousness as an English term or else used deliberately, as by Kindred, 'to emphasise that the French institution has no English or American counterpart'[19] – is meaningless, it is not at all obvious how the French term should be translated in general contexts where it is not just the institution's prosecution functions that are being discussed or referred to. 'Crown Office' (on the Scottish model) is plainly inappropriate for a republic (and means something quite different in England in any case), while 'State Office' does not really convey any clear meaning at all. The only possible rendering seems to be 'State Counsel's Office'; failing which the term must probably be transcribed and glossed.[20]

18. *Commissaire du gouvernement* is also, however, the title of the head of the *ministère public* in military courts, where he is assisted by one or more *substituts*; he is usually a civil *magistrat* on secondment and is answerable to the minister responsible for the armed forces. More importantly, there are also quite different officials with the same title in the administrative divisions of the Conseil d'État. These are senior civil servants who do represent government departments and are responsible for putting forward government views and projects; as such, they are ministerial spokesmen and not members of the Conseil d'État.

19. René David, *French Law. Its Structure, Sources, and Methodology* (Louisiana State University Press, 1972), p. 59, translator's note.

20. In particular, 'State Counsel's Office' is more concrete and specific than

This translation will also do for *magistrature debout* and *parquet* as these two terms are synonymous with *ministère public* to the extent that all three terms refer to the same external reality, the same institution; and in most texts of a legal nature, that will be all that matters. Obviously, though, each French term represents a different way of looking at the same institution and draws attention to different aspects of it: the staff of State Counsel's Office are described collectively as the *magistrature debout* because, although when appearing in court they are – strikingly, to English eyes – seated on the same level as the judges, they have to stand in order to make their submissions to the court. The term *parquet* – originally meaning 'well of the court' and later, by extension, the part of the court building occupied by State Counsel's Office – derives from the historical fact that the King's representatives originally pleaded from the bar and not from the judges' dais as is the practice today.[21]

From what precedes, it will also be evident that *officier du ministère public* can be rendered simply as 'member of State Counsel's Office'.

Procureur général is for some unknown reason frequently translated as 'Attorney-General' and occasionally as 'Director of Public Prosecutions', which is more often offered as a translation of *procureur de la République*, however. It cannot be sufficiently stressed that these are quite unacceptably inaccurate and misleading translations: quite apart from the fact that there is effectively only one Attorney-General and one Director of Public Prosecutions in the English legal system whereas in France there is a *procureur général* attached to the Court of Cassation, to the Audit Court and to each court of appeal and a *procureur de la République* at every Tribunal de Grande Instance, the Attorney-General is a political appointee and the Director is concerned only with criminal proceedings; furthermore, both generally act only in cases of some national importance, whereas *procureurs généraux* act as a matter of course in the courts to which they are attached. A commoner translation of *procureur de la République* is 'public prosecutor' (or 'State prosecutor'), which, as

---

ministère public and is accordingly quite inadequate for translating the French term in expressions such as 'Auprès du tribunal de grande instance, le ministère public est assuré par le procureur de la République', where one might possibly translate as '. . . the State is represented by . . .'.

21. As a matter of usage, however, *parquet* seems to be the term preferred before trial (e.g. *déférer quelqu'un au parquet* – 'bring someone before the public prosecutor'), while *ministère public* is used during trial (*le réquisitoire du ministère public* – usually 'the prosecution's address to the court (in which it seeks a specified sentence)', but see also note 11 on p. [130] below).

implied earlier, would be quite acceptable in the context solely of criminal proceedings (with *procureur général* being rendered as 'Principal Public Prosecutor' or 'Chief Public Prosecutor').[22] Another possible solution is to take over the Scottish term and use 'procurator' for *procureur de la République* and 'Procurator-General' for *procureur général*, but I have not seen this done, and the terms sound a little quaint to the English ear.[23] A better suggestion, where *ministère public* is to be translated as 'State Counsel's Office', would be to render *procureur de la République* as 'State Counsel' and *procureur général* as 'Principal State Counsel' (whose department is occasionally referred to as the *parquet général*, which can be translated as 'Principal State Counsel's Office').[24] *Substitut général* could then be translated as 'Assistant Principal State Counsel'.[25] *Procureur adjoint* would become 'Deputy State Counsel', *premier substitut* 'Senior Assistant State Counsel', and *substitut* 'Assistant State Counsel'. Again, the only alternative would seem to be to transcribe and gloss – although it is worth pointing out that it will by no means always be necessary in translation to make all the above fine distinctions of rank.

It should now be clear why *magistrat* cannot properly be translated simply as 'judge' nor *magistrature* as 'judiciary'. The *magistrature* also comprises the *ministère public* and some officials at the Ministry of Justice (the departments of which are commonly known collectively as the *Chancellerie*, though this meaning of *chancellerie* is curiously absent from *Harrap's New Standard French and English Dictionary*); at the same time (in its strict sense) it excludes the judges (and most Government Commissioners) of the administrative courts. The term is consequently more or less un-

22. 'Chief Crown Prosecutor' and 'Crown Prosecutor' are the titles of members of the Crown Prosecution Service in England.

23. There is in fact nominally still an English office of H. M. Procurator-General, held, along with the slightly less obscure office of Queen's Proctor ('procurator' and 'proctor' are of course cognate), by the Treasury Solicitor.

24. Cf. Principal Crown Counsel, Senior Crown Counsel and Crown Counsel in the Mauritian system, where the former *procureur général* and his *substituts* were replaced in 1957 by an Attorney-General, a Solicitor-General and a Director of Public Prosecutions, who all perform functions similar to those of their English counterparts. The Crown Counsel, however, correspond more to the *procureurs* of the French system (though they usually work *either* to the Attorney-General through the Solicitor-General on purely civil matters *or* to the Director of Public Prosecutions on criminal cases). The department, known up to 1957 as the *parquet*, was renamed the Crown Law Office, though keeping the civil-law functions of the *ministère public* – a term which has been retained untranslated.

25. Cf. 'Principal Crown Counsel' and 'Assistant Principal Crown Counsel' in Hong Kong.

translatable into English. For most purposes, however, 'judicial authorities' or 'national legal service' will serve as a translation; alternatively, one must enumerate (or transcribe and gloss) as, say, 'ordinary-court judges, members of State Counsel's Offices and certain officials at the Ministry of Justice'. *Magistrat* is, if anything, even less translatable – perhaps 'judicial officer' might do on occasion, but it is of uncertain reference, and generally one will have to enumerate (or transcribe and gloss) as 'ordinary-court judge, member of State Counsel's Office or official at the Ministry of Justice'. Appearing after an individual's name as an indication of his status, it must be adopted in English, as often with the other legal professions mentioned in Section 7.1.[26]

7.3 Academic lawyers

This chapter on the personnel of the law should not close without mention of the rôle played by those other important personages of French law, the university professors and other academic writers.

Although the courts of France are in practice (albeit behind the façade of statutory interpretation) no less creative than those of England and probably more so, the English judicial function of discursively explaining and developing the law through argument and counter-argument is performed in France not by the judiciary but by, on the one hand, legal scholars and, on the other, those members of collegiate courts who are responsible for drawing up reasoned proposals for a decision in any given case, barristers and other professional lawyers, and the members of State Counsel's Office in their submissions to the courts; it is often through the last-mentioned channel that academic writing influences the development of case-law.[27]

It is in fact primarily the legal scholars that expound the law and

26. *Magistrat* does also have the much broader generic (and non-legal) meaning of 'person in authority'. Thus a mayor may be referred to as *le premier magistrat de la ville* or the French President as *le premier magistrat de France*. Needless to say, the meaning here is *not* 'the senior law officer/judge of . . .'! In cases where the expressions cannot be translated simply as 'the mayor of . . .' or 'the President of France', the term will have to be rendered as 'officer' or 'authority' or some equivalent.

27. In their personal, argumentative, discursive style the submissions of State Counsel resemble English judgments far more than do French judgments, which are impersonal and terse in the extreme – so much so, that it is often only thanks to learned annotation by some distinguished legal scholar that it is at all clear whether a given decision affirms, modifies or departs from previous case-law (*jurisprudence*).

do the basic thinking for the whole of the legal fraternity.[28] Hence, as in Germany and Italy too, the leading law professors and lecturers in France enjoy a much more prestigious position in the hierarchy of the legal profession than either their counterparts in England or judges in France (other than the members of the two supreme courts); their names are often more familiar to the public than those of any other lawyers apart from a few conspicuous members of the bar, whereas judges in particular are almost as anonymous as civil servants in England.[29] Some university teachers also practise as barristers, but even from those who do not litigants often seek advisory opinions for submission to the courts in support of their cases, and this practice narrows the gap between lecture-room and court as well as enhancing the teacher's status. There is also a tradition that one of the judges both of the Court of Cassation and of the Conseil d'État is a law professor.

It is true that in England, contrary to earlier practice, legal textbooks are increasingly cited not only to courts in argument but also (which does not happen in France) by courts in their judgments; but the prestige of legal writers in France is both greater and of much longer standing. The writings of such scholars – textbooks, annotated law reports, articles in learned journals, etc. – have been referred to as *la doctrine* since the nineteenth century, when the more progressive jurists realised the absurdity of trying to maintain opinions that the courts were determined to reject and accordingly set about building up a new body of writing based on case-law. *Doctrine* thus 'signifies the body of opinions on legal

---

Such annotation is the more necessary as the judgment of a French court (as of the Criminal Division of the English Court of Appeal) is the collective judgment of the court as a whole, with no separate dissenting (or, come to that, concurring) opinions being given.

28. It is worth pointing out here that whereas 'lawyer' in English implies primarily a legal *practitioner* (so that the adjective 'academic' has to be added if one wants to refer solely to university teachers of law, as in the title of this section), the apparently equivalent French word *juriste* has no such necessary connotation. On the contrary, it evokes primarily the idea of a person academically qualified in the law, who is as likely to be a legal scholar as to be a practitioner, and thus corresponds more closely to 'jurist' (in British usage), though that word is relatively little used; and the French term *homme de loi*, which necessarily implies a practitioner, is arguably a closer referential equivalent of the English term 'lawyer', but it is much less commonly used than either *juriste* in French or 'lawyer' in English (though it is used, for example, by Guillien and Vincent in the quotation from their dictionary in the first paragraph of this chapter).

29. Numbers are again no doubt also relevant to the matter of prestige: as was pointed out at the beginning of Section 7.2, there are perhaps three times as many full-time judges in France as in England.

matters expressed in books and articles. The word is also used to characterise collectively the persons engaged in this analysis, synthesis and evaluation of legal source materials, members of the legal professions who devote substantial attention to scholarly work and acquire reputations as authorities'.[30] Given this dual meaning, the word – a notorious *faux ami*, like *jurisprudence* mentioned in note 27 above – would seem to be best translated (where, as usually in legal contexts, it does not mean 'doctrine') as 'legal writers/scholars' or 'legal writing/scholarship', though often 'the literature' or 'the textbooks' or 'the writings of legal scholars' or 'academic opinion' will also suit different contexts.

30. H. P. de Vries, *Civil Law and the Anglo-American Lawyer* (Oceana Publications, 1976), p. 300.

–8–

The investigation, prosecution and punishment of crime

8.1 Classification of offences

Criminal offences in France are divided into three categories: in ascending order of gravity, *contraventions* (themselves subdivided into five classes), which are tried by the police court; *délits*, which are tried by the Criminal Court; and *crimes*, which are tried by the Assize Court. These distinctions do not correspond to the one current in England until 1967 between felonies and misdemeanours, and those terms are in any case now obsolete (having been replaced by a classification into 'arrestable' and 'non-arrestable' offences – again a bipartite classification, not a tripartite one). Translation can accordingly only provide some semantic equivalence, and there are several possible classifications which could be adopted, the essential requirement being total consistency within any one text. This is also clearly a case where it would be desirable to give the original French term in brackets on the first occasion when the translation is used.

The set of terms used by Kindred in René David's *French Law* – 'minor offence', 'intermediate offence' and 'major offence' – has the merit of simplicity and using only a single noun ('offence'), but 'intermediate offence' perhaps sounds a little odd and is not wholly transparent in meaning, while the overtones of *crime* (cf. *crime contre l'humanité*, etc.) are lost. Walker suggests (on p. 315 of his *Oxford Companion to Law*) the terms 'petty offence', 'major offence' and 'serious crime'. This seems more satisfactory, but 'major offence' would be better balanced by 'minor offence' than by 'petty offence' (which would be the antonym rather of 'serious offence'). The best solution might therefore be: 'minor offence', 'major offence' and 'serious crime', though clearly mention of 'major offences' on their own (without the French in brackets) could mistakenly be taken to subsume *crimes* as well – in which case a different rendering would have to be adopted for *délits*, such as 'more serious offences', according to context; and *crimes et délits*, for instance, might be translated as 'serious crimes and other major offences'.

Two further points should be noted. Firstly, there is no legal distinction in English between 'offence' and 'crime': the latter generally denotes a more serious offence in common parlance, while 'offence' is largely a technical word other than in the collocation 'traffic offence'; and secondly, as regards method of trial the English legal system adopts another bipartite classification rather than a tripartite one like the French one, namely into 'summary' and 'indictable' offences. Thus in texts where only one or two of the French terms occur, and not the whole set, the specifically English terms 'summary offence' (as also 'petty offence') could be used for *contravention*, while *délits* and *crimes* could be jointly covered by 'indictable offences' (or, less technically, 'serious offences'); but as the distinctions and procedures are not identical, it is probably better to avoid technical English translations here.

8.2 Reporting an offence

As in England, most criminal offences will in France be reported in the first instance to the police. Alternatively, they may be reported direct to the local public prosecutor, who is responsible for the prosecution of all serious offences (*délits* and *crimes*) on the basis of information laid by either the police or a private citizen. If the offence is reported by a victim or other aggrieved party, the relevant term used is *porter plainte*; if by a third party, *dénoncer*. In cases where an offence has been reported to the police (which for the purposes of this chapter should be understood as including the gendarmerie), these terms can both be rendered in English (where the distinction dependent on whether the person reporting the offence is or is not an aggrieved party does not apply) as 'report (an offence, etc.) to the police'. If the offence has been reported to the prosecutor, one could similarly translate as 'report . . . to the public prosecutor', but it might be as well to use a different expression in order to draw attention to the fact that the English practice of reporting an offence to the police has not applied. Bearing in mind not only the expression 'to report an offence to the police' but also the more technical terms 'to lay an information' (before justices – i.e. magistrates – exercising their criminal jurisdiction) and 'to make a complaint' (to justices exercising their civil jurisdiction), one might perhaps suggest 'lodge a complaint (with the public prosecutor) (alleging . . .)' where the complainant is a member of the public and 'lay an information (against someone)' in the case of a police complaint.

Diagram 8.1 Pre-trial criminal procedure

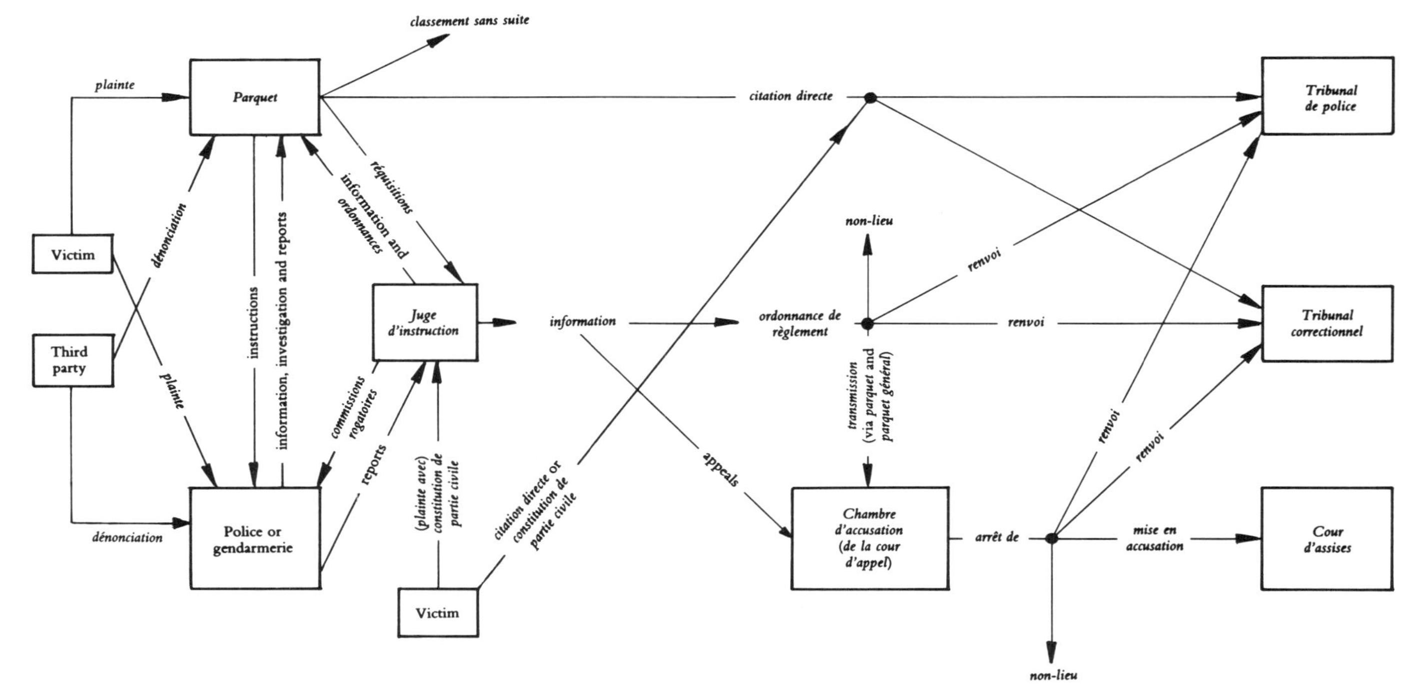

8.3 Police investigation and the public prosecutor's disposal

Whether an offence has been reported to the police or to the prosecutor (or uncovered by the police themselves), the police will usually – either on their own initiative or on the instructions of the prosecutor, but at all events under the latter's direction – carry out an *enquête préliminaire*, a procedure which can normally be translated simply as 'investigation' or 'inquiries', unless it is not clear in the context that it is the police investigation which is meant, not the judicial investigation to be mentioned in the next section (the word *préliminaire* means preliminary not to any trial but to the prosecutor's decision on how to dispose of the case). Where a serious crime or other major offence punishable by imprisonment has been committed, an investigation may be upgraded to an *enquête de flagrant délit*. This is a difficult term to translate as the procedure covers *crimes* as well as *délits* and has long since ceased to apply solely to offenders caught in the act of committing an offence but is employed in a number of other circumstances, for example where the perpetrator of the offence is followed by a hue and cry or where, shortly after the offence has been committed, the suspect is found in possession of articles (weapons, proceeds of robbery, etc.), or to be bearing traces, which suggest a connection with the offence. Since the main effect of this classification is to increase the powers of the police and the prosecutor in relation to the particular offence and allow of a more summary procedure, the translation 'expedited (police) investigation' may tentatively be suggested.

The usual range of powers available to the police includes *garde à vue* ('police custody') – the holding of a suspect or other person at a police station in order that he may 'help the police with their inquiries'. Such detention can be ordered only by a senior officer and where the offence is punishable by imprisonment. After twenty-four hours, the prosecutor (before whom, other than in expedited investigations, the detainee must normally have been produced) may give written authorisation for the person concerned to be held in custody for a further twenty-four hours; a total period of up to four days may be authorised by the prosecutor and, as the case may be, the President of the Tribunal de Grande Instance or the *juge d'instruction* (see next section) in respect of terrorist offences or by the prosecutor alone in respect of drug offences.

Once the police investigation has been completed, the papers are sent to the prosecutor, who has almost complete discretion as to the action to be taken next – in particular whether or not to prosecute.

This fundamental discretion is referred to as the principle of the *opportunité des poursuites*, literally the 'advisability of prosecuting' but probably best translated in most contexts as '(the principle of) discretionary prosecution' or simply 'the discretionary principle'; as always, however, the translator must be free to translate as stylistically appropriate in the context of a given sentence: in English a verb and an adjective are natural in many cases where, as here, French uses nouns linked by a preposition, e.g. 'The principle that prosecution is discretionary . . .', 'As prosecution is discretionary . . .'.[1] While *poursuite(s)* is the general word for prosecution, the specific term for a public prosecution initiated by the public prosecutor is *action publique*, and *déclencher* (or, more accurately, *exercer* or *engager*) *l'action publique* means 'prosecute', 'bring a prosecution', 'institute (criminal) proceedings'; occasionally (and more fittingly), where it is the victim who triggers the procedure in circumstances to be mentioned in a moment, *déclencher l'action publique* means 'bring about a public prosecution'.

The prosecutor accordingly has a number of choices open to him. If it has proved impossible to discover the identity of the person responsible for a relatively minor offence, or if the matter complained of does not in law amount to a criminal offence, or if there is not enough evidence to secure a conviction, or if for any other good reason it appears inappropriate to proceed, the prosecutor may opt for *classement sans suite*, i.e. decide to discontinue the proceedings or drop the case. (This does not preclude the file's being reopened if, for example, fresh evidence comes to light and the limitation period of the offence in question has not run out.) This course is adopted in a third or more of cases. The prosecutor's discretion is not unlimited, however. Thus, on the one hand, he may be ordered to bring a prosecution by his superior, the Principal Public Prosecutor at the Court of Appeal; while, on the other, he cannot prosecute in some cases (notably in respect of certain family matters) unless the victim has made a formal complaint to the police or the prosecutor.

In straightforward cases in which a *contravention* or a *délit* has allegedly been committed by an identified person living at a known

1. The opposite principle is that of the *légalité des poursuites*, a *faux ami* which means not the lawfulness of prosecution but the principle that prosecution of all offences is mandatory by law – 'the principle of mandatory prosecution', 'the mandatory principle'. It may be noted in passing that the *opportunité* of an administrative decision is its advisability in the sense of its merits and would probably be termed in English judicial contexts either 'the way the authority, etc., had exercised its discretion' or occasionally simply 'policy'.

address, the prosecutor will usually bring proceedings in the police court or the Criminal Court as appropriate. This will commonly be done by means of *citation directe* – having a bailiff serve a *citation à comparaître* ('summons (to appear)'). The word *directe* signifies merely that the presumed offender is being brought before the court direct without any prior judicial investigation.

It should be pointed out here that if the prosecutor has declined to proceed, the victim may (acting through a barrister) likewise issue a summons, thus in effect bringing a private prosecution – a term which may sometimes be apt to translate *citation directe* in such a case; this step will force the public prosecutor's hand and trigger a public prosecution, in which (criminal) proceedings the victim will be a civil party seeking damages for the harm suffered as a direct result of the alleged offence.[2] If the public prosecutor has already set a prosecution in motion, the victim may still apply to the court to join the proceedings as a civil party seeking damages, a procedure termed *constitution de partie civile*, the civil action being known as the *action civile*.

Where a *crime* has been committed or where a *délit* (or, very rarely, a *contravention*) has been committed either by an unknown person or in complex circumstances, the prosecutor will normally transfer the case to the *juge d'instruction*, whose rôle is described in the next section. This he will do by means of a *réquisitoire introductif*, otherwise known as a *réquisitoire à fin d'informer*; both terms may be translated as '(prosecutor's) application for a judicial investigation'.

However, if the prosecutor wishes to avoid what in cases of *crime* is an absolute obligation to hand over to the *juge d'instruction* it is open to him (subject to the consent of the accused and the victim) to prefer a lesser charge qualifying only as a *délit* and to bring the matter before the Criminal Court direct as described above. The 'downgrading' of the offence is known as *correctionnalisation*.

Again, where the prosecutor has declined to proceed at all, the victim may himself lodge a complaint with the *juge d'instruction* together with an application to join the proceedings as a civil party seeking damages (*plainte avec constitution de partie civile*), and this will again trigger a public prosecution.

2. In the event of an acquittal, however, the victim will bear the costs and may be liable in damages and even incur criminal liability for *dénonciation calomnieuse* ('malicious prosecution' – a criminal offence in France).

8.4 The *juge d'instruction*

The *juge d'instruction*[3] is undoubtedly the most distinctive personage in the French legal system from the point of view of a lawyer from England, where, despite the introduction of the Crown Prosecution Service, there is still no equivalent officer, as the English system of criminal justice makes no provision for any real judicial investigation of crimes. In a serious case in France, then, the *juge d'instruction* will normally be asked by the prosecutor to begin a judicial investigation (*ouvrir une information*), thus starting the process of *instruction*[4] of the case.[5]

Juges d'instruction are judges of the Criminal Division of the Tribunal de Grande Instance seconded for three years at a time for the specific purpose of conducting judicial investigations of serious offences, assembling evidence, interviewing witnesses and (where they decide that there is a case to answer) generally preparing cases for trial. Where there is more than one *juge d'instruction* at a given Tribunal de Grande Instance, the cases are allocated by that court's President. Although technically irremovable like other judges of the ordinary courts, *juges d'instruction* can be taken off the investigation of a particular case, and there have been widely publicised instances of this occurring; but in general, and notwithstanding their nickname *le petit juge*, they enjoy very wide powers – indeed, they have been described as the most powerful men in France, mainly no doubt because of their power to imprison people during their investigations. They are answerable neither to the public prosecutor nor to his superior, the Principal Public Prosecutor, and the police are at their disposal.

The function of the *juge d'instruction* is to investigate the matters set out in the prosecutor's application; while he may widen the scope of his inquiries to include any relevant persons, he may not, without seeking and obtaining a supplementary application

3. Sometimes referred to as the *magistrat instructeur* or the *juge informateur*.

4. *Information* and *instruction* (a term also used of the preliminaries to a civil trial) seem to be broadly synonymous in this context except in so far as *instruction* (especially in civil cases) appears to place greater emphasis on preparing a case for trial (cf. *instruire une affaire*, perhaps best translated as 'prepare a case'), while *information* – a term used only in criminal procedure – stresses rather the aspect of carrying out inquiries and assembling evidence.

5. Special arrangements apply in respect of juveniles, and the judicial investigation of an offence allegedly committed by a juvenile is conducted by the Juvenile Court judge. Similarly, the judicial investigation of cases triable by the High Court of Justice is carried out by five judges of the Court of Cassation, not by a *juge d'instruction*.

(*réquisitoire supplétif*) from the prosecutor, investigate other matters. He is assisted by a registrar and, in the larger courts, by a secretariat shared with colleagues. His powers and methods of investigation include the following.

Firstly, he can give orders to the police in the form of a *commission rogatoire*, for example requesting searches (*perquisitions*) to be made, persons to be questioned, property to be seized and impounded or telephones to be tapped. The term *commission rogatoire*, commonly met with in international proceedings, when it is usually translated as 'letters rogatory' (papers whereby the judicial authorities of one country ask for evidence to be taken 'on commission' in another), is in the present context better translated simply as 'instructions' where the police are concerned, but the translation 'letters rogatory' or 'request for evidence to be taken on commission' is best retained where, as is also possible, the *juge d'instruction* issues a *commission rogatoire* to a colleague in another part of the country. Strictly, however, when issued to the police in France, a *commission rogatoire* is a delegation of the judge's own powers (which are greater than those of the police, notably as regards searches) and the term may need to be translated as 'warrant'.

Secondly, the *juge d'instruction* will often order expert reports (*expertises*) to be made on technical (e.g. medical or graphological) aspects of a case. Such reports – and other similar *mesures d'instruction* ('investigative measures') – can also be applied for by the person charged, the prosecutor or a civil party and can only be refused by the judge in a formal order (*ordonnance*), in which he must state his reasons for refusing. In particular, the judge will regularly call for medical and psychiatric reports and for an *enquête sociale* ('social inquiry (report)') in respect of a person he charges.

Thirdly, he will interview and question suspects, witnesses, civil parties and other persons who can provide information. In the case of a suspect only, such interviews are termed *interrogatoires*, and at the first of them – known as the *interrogatoire de première comparution* ('first examination'[6]) – the suspect[7] will be formally told of the

6. The French term is a misnomer, since when the *juge d'instruction* charges a suspect he cannot, except in urgent cases, proceed to question him if the accused declines to make a statement without his lawyer being present.

7. A suspect is termed a *suspect* during the police investigation and up to the first examination by the judge, after which he becomes an *inculpé* for the duration of the judicial investigation. If and when he is committed for trial charged with a *contravention* or *délit* or if the case is referred to the Indictment Division, he becomes a *prévenu*; and, finally, if indicted and committed for trial at the Assizes, he is termed an *accusé*. Obviously, there are no exactly corresponding terms in English. *Inculpé*

charges against him (*inculpé* – 'charged'). The suspect cannot be charged, however, unless there is strong prima-facie evidence against him; but once such evidence exists, the judge is bound to prefer a charge or charges in order that the rights of the defence may be safeguarded, for it is only from this point on that a suspect may be assisted by a lawyer (*avocat*), who will have access to the investigation file (*dossier*[8]). If the person thus charged chooses to retain (or have assigned to him) a lawyer, the latter must be notified in advance of all subsequent examinations, which he will normally attend – though without any right to speak unless so authorised by the judge. A mere witness (which is also a suspect's status before he is charged) is not entitled to legal assistance during the judicial investigation, any more than during police inquiries, nor is a victim unless he has joined the proceedings as a civil party. Neither the charging nor the later examinations can be delegated to the police but only, where convenient (e.g. to save long, costly journeys), to another judge. Once charged, a person remains charged until the very end of the investigation, when the judge will determine whether to commit for trial or to discharge any person or persons he has earlier charged; and this applies even to those whom the investigation has subsequently shown to be innocent.

Interviews with witnesses and others are termed *auditions*, and 'examination (of)' or 'taking of evidence (from)' are better translations than 'hearing'.[9] Often, too, the judge will wish to arrange confrontations (*confrontations*) of witnesses and suspects and he may also organise a reconstruction (*reconstitution*) of the crime.

In order to secure the attendance (or the person) of those he interviews, the *juge d'instruction* (personally) can issue a variety of *mandats* ('warrants' – though, as will be seen, it will not be natural in English to translate *mandat* as 'warrant' in every case). Firstly, though the judge may initially merely send a letter to the person concerned, he can issue a *mandat de comparution*, which will be

---

may be translated as 'person charged' or possibly as 'accused', *prévenu* is best rendered as 'defendant'; and *accusé* may be either 'defendant' or (especially in discussions of criminal procedure in the abstract) 'accused'.

8. When a case comes to trial, the *dossier* (literally the case-file) will be found in many contexts to correspond in an English setting to 'the evidence'; sometimes it means simply 'case'.

9. The verb *entendre* – literally to 'hear' a person – is likewise much used in connection with criminal proceedings. Where it is the police who are taking statements from witnesses, 'take a statement (from)' is probably the best translation; and where the *juge d'instruction* is doing the interviewing, 'take evidence (from)' will usually be the most appropriate rendering. Only in the context of a trial in court is the translation 'hear (a witness)' apt.

served by a bailiff or by the police and will formally require the recipient to attend at a specified time and place. Like *citation à comparaître*, this term can be translated simply as 'summons (to appear)', since it does not authorise the use of any coercion. If it proves ineffective, however, the judge can then issue a *mandat d'amener* to the police requiring them to bring the named person before him, by force if need be. This warrant authorises the person to be held in prison for up to twenty-four hours pending the moment when he can be brought before the judge. Harrap's dictionary wrongly translates *mandat d'amener* as an 'order to offender or witness to appear (enforceable through arrest)'; the warrant is addressed to the police, not the offender, and is more simply translated in many instances as 'arrest warrant' (or 'warrant for the arrest (of)'). This, however, is the usual translation of a different warrant, the *mandat d'arrêt*, and in contexts where the distinction is important, *mandat d'amener* must be translated in another way, albeit long-windedly, e.g. 'warrant for a suspect or witness to be brought before . . .'.[10]

A *mandat d'arrêt* is issued if the whereabouts of the person sought are unknown (or if he is abroad, in which case an international warrant will be issued). Strictly, it is a warrant for both arrest and detention, since the person against whom it is made is to be taken into custody in a specified prison for a limited period pending his being brought before the judge, and it thus in effect lies half-way between a *mandat d'amener* and the *mandat de dépôt* to be considered in a moment; like the *mandat de dépôt*, it can be used only in cases concerning any *crime* or a *délit* for which the penalty is at least two years' imprisonment.

Where the judge considers it essential that a suspect who has duly appeared and is being or has been charged should not thereafter be left at liberty, he has the power – after a compulsory adversarial hearing of both the person charged (who must be assisted by his lawyer, if he has one) and the prosecutor – to issue a *mandat de dépôt* ('committal warrant'), i.e. an order addressed to the prison governor requiring him to take the person charged into custody. In the case of a *délit*, such a warrant can be issued only after an *ordonnance de mise en détention* ('detention order') has been made, setting out the reasons why detention is considered necessary. If an accused's lawyer is unavailable or the hearing cannot take place at once for some other reason, the judge may make an *ordonnance d'incarcération provisoire* ('interim detention order'), allowing the accused to be

10. There are occasions when a prosecutor too may issue such a warrant.

held for up to five days pending the hearing (but the accused must then be released if the hearing has still not taken place).

A committal warrant having been issued, the accused will thus find himself in *détention provisoire* – for an unlimited period in respect of a *crime*, and for four months in the first instance in respect of a *délit*, a period which can be successively prolonged for two or four months at a time for up to a year or, in certain circumstances, even longer. Detainees may, however, apply to the *juge d'instruction* for release at any time or be released (and possibly redetained) by him of his own motion after consultation of the prosecutor or on an application from the prosecutor; and there are other safeguards too. *Détention provisoire* is most commonly rendered as 'detention on remand' or 'remand in custody' but these are not accurate translations, partly because in England a remand is ordered by magistrates and partly because, notwithstanding the etymology of the word 'remand' and the definition given in English dictionaries, the term refers in fact to the disposal of an accused pending a later hearing of his case after an adjournment (usually so that further police inquiries can be made) and the accused is not necessarily remanded in custody, as is evidenced by the expression 'remand on bail' where the accused is admitted to bail. Since, furthermore, not all detainees will subsequently face trial, the translation 'detention pending trial' (suggested in note 4 to Chapter 4 above) is perhaps not the best either – 'pending investigation' would be nearer the truth; the simplest and most accurate rendering is probably 'pre-trial detention'.

This power to commit to prison is a not inconsiderable one – and is extensively used if one may judge from the fact that between a third and half of France's prison population is in pre-trial detention at any given time, including those actually committed for trial. In an (apparently unsuccessful) attempt to curb resort to this expedient, a new measure designed to restrict liberty rather less was introduced in 1970: *contrôle judiciaire* ('judicial supervision'), which is available to the *juge d'instruction* in all cases where the offence carries a custodial penalty. The numerous possible conditions include bail (*cautionnement*), which in comparison with England is used only rarely in France. Again, a judicial supervision order may be varied or discharged by the judge.

Throughout the investigation the prosecutor is closely involved as a party; like the person or persons charged and any civil party, he may make *réquisitions* ('submissions' or 'applications'[11]) to the *juge*

11. As their etymology might suggest, there appears to be little real difference in meaning between *réquisition* and *réquisitoire*. *Réquisition* is the general word used of

d'instruction, who must in fact seek the prosecutor's view before taking any judicial decisions, and he also has the right – rarely exercised in practice – to attend all examinations and confrontations, though without being able to speak unless authorised by the judge. Under the Code of Criminal Procedure, the judge is supposed to keep the investigation proceedings confidential; and while witnesses, victims and persons charged are at liberty to make statements to the press, their lawyers must not divulge any information or document derived from the investigation file, whereas the prosecutor may issue press releases. The prosecutor, moreover, can ask to inspect the file at any time, on condition that he returns it within twenty-four hours, whereas the accused's lawyer has access to it only forty-eight hours in advance of an examination of the accused – and an unrepresented accused has no right of access to it at all.

These are some of the features of the procedure which, it must be said, contribute to its being weighted slightly in favour of the prosecution; but before the impression is created that the person charged is without recourse or that the judge has positively Draconian and unfettered powers, it should be pointed out that the accused can appeal to the Indictment Division of the Court of Appeal (see p. 82 above) against most of the judge's judicial (i.e. substantive or procedural as opposed to purely administrative) orders affecting him; and the prosecutor can appeal against all judicial orders made.[12] The Indictment Division has extensive powers and discretion on appeal; and if it considers that an investigation has gone seriously off course, it may itself take over the investigation of a case instead of remitting it to the *juge d'instruction*. In some cases a further appeal, on points of law, lies to the Court of Cassation. Furthermore, the President of the Indictment Division has supervisory duties in relation to the work of *juges d'instruction* in general and pre-trial detention in particular.

As will be seen in a moment, the Indictment Division's rôle is not confined to hearing appeals. When the *juge d'instruction* decides

---

routine applications and submissions made by the prosecutor of his own motion during the investigation, including those he is required to make before the *juge d'instruction* takes certain decisions; *réquisitoire* (in addition to being the word used to denote the prosecutor's address to a court – see note 21 on p. 114 above) is the specific name of certain applications made relating to the opening, extension or closing of an investigation.

12. A civil party's scope for appeal is more limited, but he can appeal notably against an initial *ordonnance de non-informer*, whereby a *juge d'instruction* may refuse to open an investigation (e.g. because he considers that he has no jurisdiction or that no offence has been committed) or a final *ordonnance de non-lieu* (see p. 131 below).

that his investigation is complete, he issues an *ordonnance de soit-communiqué* ('notification order' perhaps) embodying that decision and transferring the file to the public prosecutor, who must return it – within a month if an accused is in custody, otherwise within three months – together with his final application (*réquisitoire définitif*) for the judge to take specified action by way of follow-up to the investigation. (Alternatively, he may submit a *réquisitoire supplétif* requesting further investigative measures.) This step is necessary because, it should be remembered, the functions of investigator and prosecutor are distinct: the judge investigates, but prosecution is the exclusive responsibility of the prosecutor.

On receipt of the prosecutor's application (which is not, however, binding on him), or at any event when the time-limit expires, the *juge d'instruction* will make one of three possible *ordonnances de règlement* (or *ordonnances de clôture*). These terms could perhaps be translated as 'disposal order' and 'closing order' respectively.

In the first place, the judge may decide that there is no case to answer: no offence has been made out, for example, or prosecution is time-barred or precluded for other reasons (such as an amnesty or the death of the accused) or else the evidence is insufficient – or again, the person who committed the offence has never been identified. In this event, the judge will issue an *ordonnance de non-lieu*. The best translation of those offered in the dictionaries is Bridge's 'discharge' ('discharge order' might be better still). This is far superior to either 'non-suit (order)' – an obsolete expression in English law anyway – or 'dismissal of the case', both of which imply that an ordinary judge or judges have been considering evidence put before them in court, whereas 'discharge order' does not necessarily imply consideration of a case brought by others. The nearest English equivalent in sense alone might almost be 'a *nolle prosequi*', but in English law a *nolle prosequi* can be entered only by the Attorney-General, who, acting through the Director of Public Prosecutions, can theoretically intervene in any criminal proceedings in order to take over the prosecution (even if only to have the proceedings stayed, as when he enters a *nolle prosequi*). With the advent of the Crown Prosecution Service, of course, a discretion not to proceed at the outset with a prosecution initiated by the police now regularly lies with the Crown prosecutors. In the French system the equivalent of such a decision not to prosecute would, as should have become clear, be the public prosecutor's exercise of his discretion not to prosecute, rather than the *juge d'instruction*'s decision that there is no case to answer.

Most commonly, however, the *juge d'instruction* will issue an *ordonnance de renvoi* ('committal for trial', 'order committing for trial', *not* 'committal order', which suggests committal to prison – cf. the translation offered for *mandat de dépôt* above), committing the accused for trial at the Criminal Court or (rarely) the police court; or, in the less frequent case of a *crime*, an *ordonnance de transmission* (*de pièces*) (*au procureur général*) ('transfer order'), transferring the case via the prosecutor to the Principal Public Prosecutor for submission to the Indictment Division of the Court of Appeal for (compulsory) further examination and a final decision on whether or not to indict the accused and send him for trial at the Assize Court. After its examination of such a case, the Indictment Division will itself then deliver one of three *arrêts* ('judgments'): an *arrêt de non-lieu* ('discharge'), an *arrêt de renvoi* ('committal for trial at the Criminal Court/police court') or an *arrêt de mise en accusation* ('committal for trial on indictment (at the Assize Court)'). It is only fair to add that the *juge d'instruction* will not send a case for trial or issue an order for transfer to the Principal Public Prosecutor unless he thinks it probable that the accused is indeed guilty; and this may explain why there are relatively few acquittals by assize courts in particular.

It will be seen that the rôle of the *juge d'instruction* bears little or no real resemblance to that of the English examining magistrate in committal proceedings – and yet *juge d'instruction* is, in the press especially, widely (mis)translated as 'examining magistrate'. Committal proceedings before magistrates are usually fairly summary and take place in court, whereas the *juge d'instruction* normally has a much longer task and plays a thoroughgoing investigative rôle, working from his office. More importantly, perhaps, he is a full-time professional judge, not an unpaid lay magistrate. Given these considerations, the best translation – as has more or less emerged naturally during the discussion of the judge's rôle – is 'investigating judge', though 'examining magistrate' may by now be too entrenched as a translation to be displaced.

French pre-trial criminal procedure is, as even this short account will probably have made plain, a sophisticated and complex system which has the advantages of thoroughness and – since more preparation (and, importantly, investigation) of the case is done by a State-paid judge and less by fee-earning counsel in private practice – relative inexpense for the parties (both prosecution and defence) but the drawbacks of slowness and excessive use of pre-trial detention. Over the past twenty years there have been numerous attempts at reform of the system in general and of pre-trial detention in particular (for example by removing the power to commit from the single investigating judge and vesting it in a panel of three judges), and some of these reforms have even reached the statute book, only to be repealed before they came into force, mainly for practical reasons such as staffing problems, most recently again in 1989.

Trial procedure in the various courts is of course, in an essentially inquisitorial system of criminal justice, somewhat different from that in English courts, but not so markedly as to be an obvious source of terminological difficulty once the background set out in the foregoing sections and chapters is familiar. It would accordingly be inappropriate in a limited study such as this to describe it, and the final section in this chapter will give merely a very brief survey of the main penalties and disposals available to French criminal courts at the end of a trial.

8.5 Sentences

Judgment in the French Criminal Court and the police court may be *mis en délibéré* ('reserved'), but sooner or later it will be delivered. Not every trial, of course, will end in a conviction: the accused may be (in the police court or the Criminal Court) *relaxé* or (at the Assizes) *acquitté*. Both those words mean 'acquitted', as does a less common term (often mistranslated) which can be used of an acquittal in any court, *renvoyé des fins de la poursuite*.[13]

More often than not, however, there will be a *condamnation*. The translation of this word requires care. Strictly, it means 'conviction and sentence' and occasionally it has to be so translated, but in most linguistic contexts it usually corresponds to *either* 'conviction' *or* 'sentence' in English, for example *condamnation pour vol* ('conviction for theft') but *condamnation à vie* ('life sentence'), while *purger une condamnation* would have to be translated in the same way as *purger une peine* ('serve a sentence'). Whereas *peine* corresponds to the 'sentence' part of the meaning of *condamnation*, there is no separate French word corresponding to just the 'conviction' part, for which *condamnation* therefore has to do duty too.

Just as not every trial ends in a conviction, so a conviction will not necessarily entail a sentence. There are two similar terms to

13. The translation of *relaxe* (meaning 'acquittal') offered by Harrap's dictionary – 'release (of prisoner') – is misleading, and there seems to be no justification whatever for the alternative rendering given, 'order of *nolle prosequi*' (cf. p. 131 above). Release or discharge of the prisoner is what follows as a *consequence* of an acquittal – and release can occur in other circumstances too.

note here: *absolution* and *dispense de peine. Absolution* is the exemption from punishment which in certain circumstances normally follows if one or more statutory grounds for exemption (*excuses absolutoires*) apply in a given case (e.g. where a person convicted of conspiracy has prevented the commission of the planned crime); it covers only *peines principales* (see below) and does not preclude the imposition of other, lesser penalties. It is important to realise that *absolution* is therefore not an acquittal (a translation given by the Harrap and the Herbst and Readett dictionaries), and the best translation would probably be 'statutory exemption from punishment'. *Dispense de peine*, on the other hand, can be given only in respect of *contraventions* and *délits* and is a judicial act of clemency corresponding to the English 'absolute discharge', as, while there is a finding (and declaration) of guilt, no punishment whatever is imposed nor, technically, is there any conviction.

In the ordinary case, however, there will be a sentence, and the main types of *peine* ('sentence', 'penalty' or 'punishment') will now be summarised (no attempt will be made to indicate the precise punishments for particular offences or to list all the available penalties exhaustively). Sentences are classified in several different ways, some of which – as seems to be quite often the case in French law! – are of almost entirely theoretical interest. Only the basic categorisations will be mentioned here.

Firstly, penalties are classified purely formally according to the category of the offence (the classification of offences was described in Section 8.1 above). The penalty for a *crime* is a *peine criminelle*; for a *délit*, a *peine correctionnelle*; and for a *contravention*, a *peine de police*. Clearly, as these terms correspond purely formally to a set of terms which themselves have no formal equivalent in English, they cannot be translated other than by 'penalty for serious crimes' and so on.

Within each of those categories, penalties are *principales* ('primary' or 'principal'), *accessoires* ('ancillary' or 'accessory') or *complémentaires* ('additional'). Ancillary punishments automatically accompany the primary penalty, whether explicitly mentioned in the sentence or not. In some circumstances they may be imposed in lieu of a primary penalty. Any additional penalties (some of which are mandatory and some optional) have to be imposed in express terms.

The following are the primary penalties for each category of offence.

The penalties for *crimes* are subdivided into *peines afflictives et infamantes* and *peines infamantes*. These again have no equivalent in

English and are difficult to translate at all naturally. One method is to define rather than translate the terms, e.g. '(penalties entailing) imprisonment and loss of civic rights' and '(penalties entailing) loss of civic rights' respectively. That, however, does not convey the meaning of the French words actually used, and would be a useless procedure in a text which went on to define the penalties in French (the only sort of text in which one is in fact ever likely to encounter the terms), so it would be more sensible to opt for a literal translation, however unnatural-sounding to English ears. *Afflictive* describes a penalty which has physical (e.g. restraining) effects on the person (including termination of his life, although the death penalty was abolished in France in 1981), while *infamante* means 'dishonouring'; accordingly, one might suggest 'dishonouring penalties entailing physical restraint'[14] and 'dishonouring penalties'[15] respectively. The penalties in the former category are *réclusion criminelle à perpétuité* ('life imprisonment'[16]) and *réclusion criminelle à temps* ('fixed-term imprisonment', 'determinate sentence of imprisonment') for ordinary crimes and *détention criminelle à perpétuité* ('detention for life') and *détention criminelle à temps* ('detention for a fixed term') for political crimes. The 'dishonouring' penalties are *bannissement* ('banishment') and *dégradation civique* ('loss of civic rights'), and they are primary penalties only for political crimes; loss of civic rights is also an ancillary penalty for all ordinary crimes.

The penalties for *délits* and *contraventions* are *emprisonnement* ('imprisonment') and *amende* ('fine').

As to substance or nature, penalties are in English terms essentially either custodial or non-custodial. As the reader would expect

14. In their book *Sanctions-Systems in the Member-States of the Council of Europe* (Kluwer Law and Taxation Publishers 1988–), p. 102, A. M. van Kalmthout and P. J. P. Tak use the term 'corporal punishment' for *peine afflictive*. This will not do at all, as corporal punishment implies infliction of physical pain, being associated with caning (in schools) or birching and flogging (as criminal penalties).

15. Not – as Doucet's dictionary and van Kalmthout and Tak give – 'degrading': degrading treatment or punishment (*des peines ou traitements [. . .] dégradants*) is outlawed under Article 3 of the European Convention on Human Rights. The corresponding expression 'infamous punishment' formerly existed in English as a legal term.

16. Van Kalmthout and Tak, *Sanctions-Systems*, p. 74, try to distinguish between *réclusion* and *emprisonnement* (see below) by translating the former as 'confinement' and only the latter as 'imprisonment'. Like the word 'incarceration' (and the French word *incarcération*), however, 'confinement' is not used as the technical name of a punishment (except as a special kind of imprisonment, in the collocation 'solitary confinement'); it conveys nothing different from imprisonment and merely sounds odd. Both the French punishments are in any case the same in substance, so there is no point in trying to distinguish them formally in translation.

by this stage, the French classification is more refined. *Peines privatives de liberté* clearly correspond to 'custodial sentences'. Where a prison sentence of not more than six months is passed, the court may order only *semi-liberté* (which is surely more naturally rendered in English as 'semi-imprisonment' than as 'semi-liberty'), under which regime the person convicted is at liberty for purposes such as continuing to pursue an occupation, undergoing medical treatment or following a training course and must remain in prison only when not engaged in those activities. In France as in Britain, and for similar reasons, much attention has been paid in recent years to alternatives to imprisonment (initially referred to in French as *peines de substitution* but now also increasingly called *substituts à l'emprisonnement*). To traditional measures like fining or disqualification from driving in lieu of imprisonment for *délits* or *contraventions*, there has been added in the last decade *travail d'intérêt général* (or *TIG*), which corresponds to 'community service' and was introduced in 1984 under an Act of 1983.

Non-custodial sentences are divided into the following main categories.

Firstly, *peines restrictives de liberté* ('penalties restricting liberty'). The chief penalty in this category is *interdiction de séjour* ('ban on residing in (a) certain area(s)').

Secondly, *peines patrimoniales*. As these comprise both fines and confiscation (*confiscation*), the common translation 'pecuniary penalties' is not strictly accurate (and is the translation of *peines pécuniaires*); 'penalties affecting property' or even just 'property penalties' would be more exact. In certain circumstances, fines imposed on adult offenders in respect of *délits* for which the sentence could have been imprisonment may take the form of *jours-amendes* ('day-fines'), which were likewise introduced under the Act of 1983 mentioned above. Under this system the court fixes a fine to be paid daily for up to 360 days, and failure to pay at any point results in imprisonment of the offender for a number of days corresponding to half the number of unpaid day-fines.

Thirdly, *peines privatives de droits* ('penalties entailing loss of rights'). Apart from loss of civic rights (*dégradation civique*, mentioned above), these include *interdiction légale*, i.e. placing under a disability as regards the disposal of property – an ancillary penalty for all non-political *crimes*; a guardian is appointed in such cases. The term might be translated as 'statutory deprivation of right to manage property'. Other penalties are disqualification from certain professions and occupations and withdrawal of driving and other licences.

Fourthly, there is a range of measures known as *mesures de sûreté*. These include most of the measures usually applied to juvenile offenders – notably *liberté surveillée* (literally 'freedom under supervision', but corresponds fairly closely to the English 'supervision order', which sounds a more natural translation) – and other special disposals for alcoholics and drug addicts, as well as probation (see further below). The term *mesure de sûreté* strictly means 'security measure' or 'safety measure' but in this context probably corresponds more closely to a 'preventive measure'.

Lastly, in addition to the various educative measures available for juvenile offenders, mention may be made of mere *admonestation* ('reprimand').

As in English law, account will be taken, when fixing sentences, of any aggravating or extenuating circumstances. Aggravating circumstances (*circonstances aggravantes*) are all statutorily defined and must be taken into account by the court when determining sentence; extenuating circumstances may be either statutory (*excuses atténuantes*) or recognised at the discretion of the court (*circonstances atténuantes*).

Similarly, penalties imposed on certain offenders may be wholly or partly suspended. If no condition is attached, suspension (or a suspended sentence) is called *sursis* (*simple*) and may be granted only in relation to a prison sentence or fine for a *délit* or for the most serious category of *contravention*, and to one or two other penalties; thus *dix-huit mois avec sursis* would be 'an eighteen-month suspended sentence' or (less formally) 'eighteen months suspended'. The suspension is for five years. Alternatively, any offender sentenced to imprisonment for a *crime* or *délit* may have his sentence suspended conditionally: *sursis avec mise à l'épreuve* (or *sursis probatoire*) can be translated as 'probation (order)', as probation is not available in France other than as a condition of suspending some other sentence, but it corresponds more exactly to a 'suspended sentence supervision order' in England; *sursis avec* (*obligation d'accomplir un*) *travail d'intérêt général* or *sursis assorti de l'obligation d'un travail d'intérêt général* is suspension combined with a community service order. In the former case, suspension is for three to five years; in the latter case, for up to eighteen months. Lastly, in respect of any conviction for a *délit* or a *contravention* the court may in an appropriate case defer sentence, and the deferment is called *ajournement du prononcé de la peine* or simply *ajournement de peine*.

A word may be said here about the various types of prison. Leaving aside psychiatric and other hospital prisons, there are three basic kinds of institution: *maison centrale*, *centre de détention* and *maison d'arrêt*. The first of these is a closed prison for long-term prisoners and may be translated simply as 'prison' or, if necessary, 'long-stay prison'. The second is likewise for long-term prisoners but may be a closed or an open prison and has a more liberal regime emphasising resocialisation; the term is more difficult to translate, as detention centres in England are for short-term prisoners (from three weeks to four months) – perhaps 'long-term detention centre' would do. The third is a local prison mainly for prisoners in pre-trial detention, although some also take convicted prisoners who have a maximum of a year left to serve; separate wings also accommodate offenders sentenced for *contraventions*; the best translation is probably 'local prison' or possibly 'remand prison'. Prisons with wings catering for different kinds of regime are known as *centres pénitentiaires* ('prison centres'). In addition to the three basic types of prison, there are also *centres régionaux* ('regional centres') for prisoners with not more than three years to serve and *centres/quartiers de semi-liberté* ('semi-custodial centres/wings').

As in England, *libération conditionnelle* is available – i.e. 'parole' or 'release on licence' (*not* 'conditional discharge', which is a possible judicial order upon conviction of an offender and would be translated as *dispense de peine conditionnelle* in French) – as is *réduction de peine* ('remission of sentence') for good behaviour. In this context, mention should be made, lastly, of the arrangements for supervision of the serving of prison and other sentences, which is the responsibility severally of the public prosecutor's office, the Minister of Justice and, primarily, of a judge appointed for three years at a time from the Tribunal de Grande Instance, the *juge de l'application des peines* ('judge responsible for the execution of sentences'[17]). This judge chairs the *commission de l'application des peines* in each prison in the area of his court ('sentences board' perhaps) and must consult it before taking his decisions or forwarding files to the Minister for decision. He likewise chairs the *comité de probation* ('probation committee').

17. Van Kalmthout and Tak, *Sanctions-Systems*, pp. 73–87, most misleadingly refer to what must be the *juge de l'application des peines* as the 'sentencing judge'. In English law the sentencing judge is the trial judge.

Conclusion

In the foregoing pages the attempt has been made to define, and suggest solutions to, the theoretical problems of translating culture-specific concepts and the practical problems of translating into acceptable legal English the key terms used in France's legal system and in the French classification of law. It is hoped that the study will be of real practical assistance to (among others) legal translators and English-speaking students embarking on a study of French or comparative law, not only in offering translations of the terms considered in the book but also in enabling them to approach more systematically and hence more confidently the translation (or at least an understanding) of all the innumerable other terms not discussed here – and indeed of terms in other languages from other civil-law systems (though they should beware of differences in meaning between apparently corresponding terms in the various civil-law countries).

As has been seen, there *are* peculiar difficulties in this kind of translation, but – as has also been shown, I hope – they are not insuperable. Nevertheless, the research entailed in writing this book has certainly highlighted the great need for *explanatory* bilingual glossaries and dictionaries on the model of O'Rooney's excellent work, which, alas, seems to have remained without any successors.

If satisfactory legal translation into English is to be achieved, the principles expounded in Part I have to be borne in mind, because it is essential to be methodical in the approach to such translation, which, like most skills, benefits from being seen against a broader, theoretical background. Too often the wood cannot be seen for the trees, yet a knowledge of the wood is essential for identification of the trees: this is a particular occupational hazard for translators, as translation requires such close attention to formal as well as substantive detail that it is all too easy to lose sight of the purport of a text as a whole and its function in relation to its subject-matter.

Neither the English lawyer, even today still usually trained in the law of his own country alone and possessing little or no knowledge of the French language (though this is beginning to change and will have to do so fairly fast), nor the British linguist – who usually knows little of English law and nothing of French law – is equipped to translate legal French into English without further study (of French law and the French language in the lawyer's case and of English and French law in the linguist's case) and practice (in legal translation).[1] Even a lawyer with some knowledge of French and of French law will be unaccustomed to translating in general[2] and far less likely than a linguist to be on his guard against the twin dangers of language interference and of slavishly adhering to word-for-word translation where it is inappropriate, with the result that his English will often be at worst quite meaningless and at best stylistically unnatural, riddled with Gallic turns of phrase.

The kinds of error which ensue are readily found not only in texts actually translated from French – such as Kindred's version of David, from which examples have been quoted – but also in books and articles written in English about the French system, where the use that has been made of French sources all too often shines through the supposedly English text on every page.[3] An eminent British lawyer with wide experience of the civil law has publicly acknowledged that he unwittingly succumbed to the insidious danger of language interference: the recently retired President of the Court of Justice of the European Communities in Luxembourg, Lord Mackenzie Stuart, in the preface to his 1977 Hamlyn Lectures, *The European Communities and the Rule of Law*, thanks J.-P. Warner – formerly an Advocate-General at the Court of Justice, and now Mr Justice Warner of the English High Court – for having read a draft of the lectures and 'eliminated a crop of Gallicisms which had

1. Jean-Claude Gémar makes a number of pertinent comments in his article 'La traduction juridique: art ou technique d'interprétation?', *Meta*, 33 (1988), 305–19.

2. It should be emphasised that ability to do specialised translation presupposes an ability to do non-specialised translation; this is mainly because, with probably no real exceptions, specialist language does not function in isolation from ordinary language – see pp. 17–18 above. Such a presupposition is, of course, implicit in the term 'legal translator': we do not speak of 'translator lawyers'. (The Court of Justice of the European Communities, however, chooses to term its legal translators 'lawyer/linguists' – thereby seeming to emphasise that a dual formal qualification is required; but in actual fact, interestingly enough, it insists only on a formal qualification as a lawyer and is prepared to accept candidates who do *not* have any formal qualification in languages.)

3. I am, of course, making the assumption here that this is a bad thing; it has been argued by some theorists and translators in the past, however, that the translator (more particularly of literary texts) is under a duty to ensure that the form (and even the phonic substance) of the original language is reflected in the translation irrespective of whether the features concerned are natural in the TL.

insinuated themselves into the text'.[4]

It seems singularly ungracious to adduce concrete evidence of such inadequacies from an otherwise excellent book by two distinguished authors which I have read with great profit and pleasure and have drawn on extensively in my account of the administrative courts in Chapter 6; yet it is the very distinction of the authors that most convincingly makes my point that legal translation cannot safely be left to lawyers with no linguistic training. I refer to Brown and Garner's *French Administrative Law* and will illustrate two different kinds of error resulting from language interference due to the formal similarity of so many English and French words.

The first example is of a complete misunderstanding of the original French. The authors supply what purports to be a translation of the celebrated passage in the Act of 16–24 August 1790, which I have already cited in note 31 on p. 86 above. Their translation reads: 'Judicial functions are distinct and will always remain separate from administrative functions. Judges in the civil courts may not, under pain of forfeiture of their offices, concern themselves in any manner whatsoever with the operation of the administration [. . .]'.[5] Now it so happens that although the word *forfaiture* is here used in a collocation which strongly suggests that it is a penalty attaching to a certain course of behaviour on the part of judges, it is a *faux ami* and is in fact the technical term for any serious criminal offence committed by a holder of public office in the course of his duties. It could perhaps most closely be translated in general as 'criminal malfeasance in public office' or (as O'Rooney suggests) 'criminal misuse of authority by a public servant'; it does not mean 'forfeiture of office' at all (which would be *déchéance* in French), and in the present context it might simply be rendered as 'It shall be a criminal offence for the judges of the ordinary courts to . . .'.[6] The mistake is wholly understandable; but a professional translator would have been more likely to realise that he did not know the term for certain and to be wary of assuming that it meant the same as a similar-looking English term (indeed, it would be safe to assume the opposite, as such cognates are nearly always *faux amis*); he would accordingly have checked its meaning in a mono-

4. Lord Mackenzie Stuart, *The European Communities and the Rule of Law* (Stevens & Sons,1977), p. xi.

5. L. N. Brown and J. F. Garner, *French Administrative Law*, 3rd edn (Butterworths, 1983), p. 28.

6. To be scrupulously fair, 'forfeiture' in English did denote a criminal offence up to at least the time of Sir Edward Coke.

lingual dictionary. *Troubler*, on the other hand, does mean something nearer 'trouble' here and is mistranslated as 'concern themselves with'; at the least it implies 'interfere with'.

The second example is of lexical Gallicisms which are either meaningless in English or else unnatural: 'public hygiene' for 'public health' (p. 74); 'administrative reference' for *le référé administratif* (p. 75) (irrespective of its etymology, *référé* here denotes an urgent application to a judge, cf. p. 79 above); 'Code of Criminal Instruction' for 'Code of Criminal Procedure' (p. 89); 'suppression of a tramway service' for 'withdrawal of a tram service' (p. 102); 'faculties of law and letters' for 'faculties of law and arts' (p. 159); and 'autoroute' for 'motorway' (p. 160).

To redress the balance somewhat, it is worth showing how – perhaps more surprisingly – even a major English writer, who can hardly be accused of lacking linguistic awareness (in his own tongue, at any rate) has provided a striking example of the pernicious effects of such language interference in this very field. In his pamphlet *J'Accuse* published in 1982 Graham Greene commits many enormities in the way of Gallicisms, some of them quite meaningless in English. Examples are 'infractions' (i.e. offences) (p. 14), 'pursued for receipt of stolen goods' (prosecuted for receiving) (p. 18), 'proofs' (i.e. evidence) (p. 29) and 'condemnations' (i.e. convictions) (p. 33). Though technically 'legal', none of the proper English terms is so specialised as to be outside the average educated English-speaker's vocabulary. Nor does it seem possible that the Gallicisms are being deliberately used to provide local colour, since the pamphlet is not (ostensibly, at any rate) a work of fiction and the terms are not obviously Gallic (as opposed to just odd) to the uninitiated reader. Amid the controversy over the pamphlet's content, these matters of expression seem to have gone unremarked, though it is difficult to imagine that anyone – let alone a linguist or a novelist – could fail to be struck by them. Since such peculiarities are not, to my knowledge, apparent in Greene's novels (evidence that has been pointed out to me in his recent work is inconclusive), one can only surmise that whereas the novels reflect personal experience at most very indirectly, *J'Accuse* purports to retell a true story, which must have been learnt about from first-hand written and oral reports *in French*. These, presumably, were then unconsciously transposed word for word (instead of consciously translated) into English when Greene wrote up his own account.

People qualified both as lawyers and as linguists are, in common-law countries at least, still fairly few in number and are much more likely to practise as lawyers than as translators. Even if they do take up translation, neither their legal nor their linguistic training will necessarily have imparted, as required, a knowledge of the relevant foreign law and/or legal system. H. C. Gutteridge is worth quoting at the end of this book as at the beginning:

> The isolation of legal thought in national watertight compartments has always seemed to me to be one of the factors which is most prolific in producing that frame of mind which leads to a spirit of national egotism. We have much to learn from one another in legal as well as other departments of human activities, and it is, in a sense, a reproach to the lawyers of all nations that they have been unable, up to the present, to arrive at the free interchange of knowledge and ideas which has been attained in other branches of learning.[7]

Fortunately there are signs that things are changing, a process that began perhaps soon after Britain's accession to the European Community in 1973.[8] In so far as mutual ignorance does still prevail, it is probably now due primarily to language barriers; and one aim of this study has been to make a small contribution to breaking down such barriers between lawyers from different countries and legal systems.

7. H. C. Gutteridge, 'The comparative aspects of legal terminology', *Tulane Law Review*, 12 (1938), 401–11 (p. 410).

8. Inevitably one thinks of Lord Denning's oft-quoted and far-sighted words early on in the post-accession era, in the case of *H. P. Bulmer Ltd* v. *Bollinger SA* ([1974] All ER 1226), where, speaking of the Treaty of Rome, he said: '[W]hen we come to matters with a European element, the Treaty is like an incoming tide. It flows into the estuaries and up the rivers. It cannot be held back.'

Bibliography

The most directly relevant and useful introductory books and articles are marked with an asterisk.

A. Linguistics and translation theory

Berry, M., *Introduction to Systemic Linguistics*, 2 vols (Batsford, 1975–7)

Brislin, R. W., ed., *Translation. Applications and Research* (Gardner Press, 1976)

*Catford, J. C., *A Linguistic Theory of Translation* (Oxford University Press, 1965)

Crystal, D., and D. Davy, *Investigating English Style* (Longman, 1969)

*Darbelnet, J., 'Réflexions sur le discours juridique', *Meta*, 24 (1979), 26–34

*Delisle, J., *L'Analyse du discours comme méthode de traduction* (Éditions de l'Université d'Ottawa, 1980)

Ellis, J., and J. N. Ure, 'Registers', in A. R. Meetham et al., eds, *Encyclopaedia of Linguistics, Information and Control* (Pergamon, 1969), pp. 251–9; reprinted in abridged form in C. S. Butler and R. R. K. Hartmann, eds, *A Reader on Language Variety* (University of Exeter, 1976, repr. 1979)

*Gémar, J.-C., 'La traduction juridique et son enseignement: aspects théoriques et pratiques', *Meta*, 24 (1979), 35–53

*——, 'La traduction juridique: art ou technique d'interprétation?', *Meta*, 33 (1988), 305–19

——, ed., *Langage du droit et traduction. Essais de jurilinguistique. The Language of the Law and Translation. Essays on Jurilinguistics* (Linguatech/ Conseil de la langue française, 1982)

Groot, G. R. de, 'Problems of legal translation from the point of view of a comparative lawyer', in P. H. M. Gerver, E. H. Hondius and G. J. W. Steenhoff, eds, *Netherlands Reports to the Twelfth International Congress of Comparative Law, Sydney–Melbourne 1986* (T. M. C. Asser Instituut, 1987), pp. 1–19

Haas, W., 'The theory of translation', *Philosophy*, 37 (1962), 208–28; reprinted in G. H. R. Parkinson, ed., *The Theory of Meaning* (Oxford University Press, 1968), pp. 86–108

Halliday, M. A. K., and R. Hasan, *Cohesion in English* (Longman, 1976)

*Halliday, M. A. K., A. McIntosh and P. D. Strevens, *The Linguistic Sciences and Language Teaching* (Longman, 1964)

*Koller, W., *Einführung in die Übersetzungswissenschaft*, 3rd edn (Quelle & Meyer, 1987)

*Lane, A., 'Quelques aspects de la terminologie juridique et administrative', *Babel*, 15 (1969), 31–6

Lauzière, L., 'Un Vocabulaire juridique bilingue canadien', *Meta*, 24 (1979), 109–14

Lyons, J., *Semantics*, 2 vols (Cambridge University Press, 1977)

*Meredith, R. C., 'Some notes on English Legal Translation', *Meta*, 24 (1979), 68–94

Mounin, G., *Les Problèmes théoriques de la traduction* (Gallimard, 1963)

——, *Linguistique et traduction* (Dessart et Mardaga, 1976)

——, 'La linguistique comme science auxiliaire dans les disciplines juridiques', *Meta*, 24 (1979), 9–17

*Newmark, P. P., 'Twenty-three restricted rules of translation', *Incorporated Linguist*, 12 (1973), 9–15

——, 'The theory and craft of translation', *Language Teaching and Linguistics Abstracts*, 9 (1976), 5–26

*——, 'The translation of proper names and institutional and cultural terms', *Incorporated Linguist*, 16 (1977), 59–63; reprinted in revised and expanded form in Newmark, *Approaches to Translation*, pp. 70–83

——, *Approaches to Translation* (Pergamon, 1981)

*——, 'Jean Delisle's theory of translation', *Incorporated Linguist*, 22 (1983), 136–8

*——, *A Textbook of Translation* (Prentice Hall, 1988)

Nida, E. A., *Toward a Science of Translating* (Brill, 1964)

——, and W. D. Reyburn, *Meaning across Cultures* (Orbis, 1981)

——, and C. R. Taber, *The Theory and Practice of Translation* (Brill, 1969, repr. 1974)

Quirk, R., et al., *A Grammar of Contemporary English* (Longman, 1972, repr. 1979)

Reid, T. B. W., 'Linguistics, structuralism and philology', *Archivum Linguisticum*, 8 (1956), 28–37

Sapir, E., *Selected Writings in Language. Culture and Personality*, D. G. Mandelbaum, ed. (University of California Press, 1949)

*Šarčević, S., 'Conceptual Dictionaries for Translation in the Field of Law', *International Journal of Lexicography*, 2 (1989), 277–93

Savory, T., *The Art of Translation*, 2nd edn (Cape, 1968)

*Sparer, M., 'Pour une dimension culturelle de la traduction juridique', *Meta*, 24 (1979), 68–94

Steiner, G., *After Babel* (Oxford University Press, 1975)

Trudgill, P., *Sociolinguistics*, 2nd edn (Penguin, 1983)

Vinay, J.-P., and J. Darbelnet, *Stylistique comparée du français et de l'anglais* (Didier, 1958, repr. 1977)

Weston, M. R., 'The role of translation at the European Court of Human Rights', in F. Matscher and H. Petzold, eds, *Protecting Human Rights: The European Dimension. Studies in honour of Gérard J. Wiarda* . . . (Carl Heymanns Verlag, 1988), pp. 679–89

Winter, H., 'Die Schokoladentorte zwickt an mir', *Frankfurter Allgemeine Zeitung*, 16 October 1981, p. 25

B. Law

Amos, Sir Maurice, and F. P. Walton, *An Introduction to French Law*, 3rd edn by F. H. Lawson, A. E. Anton and L. N. Brown (Oxford University Press, 1967)

Ancel, M., and P. Chemithe, eds, *Les Systèmes pénitentiaires en Europe occidentale* (La Documentation française, 1981)

*Aubert, J.-L., *Introduction au droit*, 5th edn (Presses Universitaires de France, 1988)

Blanc-Jouvan, X., 'Introduction à l'étude comparée des Droits de l'Océan Indien', in *Études de droit privé français et mauricien* (Presses Universitaires de France, 1969), pp. 19–33

*Bot, Y., *Les Institutions judiciaires* (Berger-Levrault, 1985)

*Brown, L. N., 'The office of the notary in France', *International and Comparative Law Quarterly*, 2 (1953), 60–71

——, 'The two legal traditions: antithesis or synthesis?', *Journal of Common Market Studies*, 18 (1979–80), 246–55

*——, and J. F. Garner, *French Administrative Law*, 3rd edn (Butterworths, 1983)

Chloros, A. G., *Codification in a Mixed Jurisdiction. The Civil and Commercial Law of Seychelles. Introduction and Texts* (North Holland Publishing Company, 1977)

*Council of Europe, *Judicial Organisation in Europe* (Morgan-Grampian, 1975)

Cross, Sir Rupert, P. A. Jones and R. Card, *Introduction to Criminal Law*, 11th edn (Butterworths, 1988)

*David, R., *French Law. Its Structure, Sources, and Methodology*, M. Kindred, trans. (Louisiana State University Press, 1972)

*——, *English Law and French Law* (Stevens & Sons and Eastern Law House, 1980)

——, and C. Jauffret-Spinosi, *Les Grands Systèmes de droit contemporains*, 9th edn (Dalloz, 1988)

——, and H. P. de Vries, *The French Legal System* (Oceana Publications, 1958)

Denning, Sir Alfred, *Freedom under the Law* (Stevens & Sons, 1949)

Dubruel de Broglio, R., 'Cours et Tribunaux (1815–1965) de l'Ile Maurice', in *Études de droit privé français et mauricien* (Presses Universitaires de France, 1969), pp. 151–63

*Fanachi, P., *La Justice administrative*, 2nd edn (Presses Universitaires de France, 1985)

Garner, J. F., 'Public and Private Law', *Law Society's Gazette*, 23 March 1983, pp. 739–40

*Gutteridge, H. C., 'The comparative aspects of legal terminology', *Tulane Law Review*, 12 (1938), 401–11

Home Office, *The Sentence of the Court*, 4th edn (HMSO, 1986, repr. 1988)

*James, P. S., *Introduction to English Law*, 12th edn (Butterworths, 1989)

*Kahn-Freund, Sir Otto, C. Lévy and B. Rudden, *A Source-book on French Law*, 2nd edn (Clarendon Press, 1979)

Kalmthout, A. M. van, and P. J. P. Tak, *Sanctions-Systems in the Member-States of the Council of Europe*, 2 vols (Kluwer Law and Taxation Publishers, 1988–)

Keith, R., and G. Clark, *A Guide to Scots Law* (Johnston and Bacon, 1978)

*Larguier, J., *Le Droit pénal*, 9th edn (Presses Universitaires de France,

*——, *La Procédure pénale*, 6th edn (Presses Universitaires de France, 1987)

——, *Droit pénal général*, 12th edn (Dalloz, 1989)

——, *Procédure pénale*, 12th edn (Dalloz, 1989)

Massot, J., and J. Marimbert, *Le Conseil d'État*, Notes et Études documentaires 4869–70 (La Documentation française, 1988)

*Merryman, J. H., *The Civil Law Tradition: an Introduction to the Legal Systems of Western Europe and Latin America*, 2nd edn (Stanford University Press, 1985)

Ministère de la Justice, *Annuaire statistique de la justice 1987* (La Documentation française, 1989)

Pinsseau, H., *L'Organisation judiciaire de la France*, Notes et Études documentaires 4777 (La Documentation française, 1985)

*Pradel, J., and L. H. Leigh, 'Le Ministère public. Examen comparé des droits anglais et français', *Revue de droit pénal et de criminologie*, 3 (1989), 223–44

*Rassat, M.-L., *La Justice en France*, 2nd edn (Presses Universitaires de France, 1987)

*Raymond, B., *Introduction to Civil and Criminal Litigation* (Oyez Publishing, 1981)

*Ruymbeke, R. van, *Le Juge d'instruction* (Presses Universitaires de France, 1988)

*Sauveplanne, J. G., *Codified and Judge Made Law* (North Holland Publishing Company, 1982)

Stuart, Lord Mackenzie, *The European Communities and the Rule of Law* (Stevens & Sons, 1977)

Vincent, J., G. Montagnier and A. Varinaud, *La Justice et ses institutions*, 2nd edn (Dalloz, 1985)

*Vries, H. P. de, *Civil Law and the Anglo-American Lawyer* (Oceana Publications, 1976)

Wade, H. W. R., *Administrative Law*, 6th edn (Oxford University Press, 1989)

*Williams, G., *Learning the Law*, 11th edn (Stevens & Sons, 1982)

Woolf, Sir Harry (Lord Justice), 'Public Law – Private Law: Why the Divide?', *Public Law* (1986), 220–38

C. Dictionaries and lexicography

Baleyte, J., et al., *Dictionnaire économique et juridique. Français–Anglais. Anglais–Français. Economic and Legal Dictionary . . .*, 2nd edn (Éditions de Navarre, 1989)

Bridge, F. H. S., ed., *The Council of Europe French–English Legal Dictionary* (Council of Europe, in press)

Burchfield, R. W., ed., *A Supplement to the Oxford English Dictionary*, 4 vols (Clarendon Press, 1972–86)

Cornu, G., ed., *Vocabulaire juridique*, 2nd edn (Presses Universitaires de France, 1990)

Council of the European Communities, General Secretariat, *European Communities Glossary, French–English. Glossaire des Communautés européennes. Français–Anglais*, 8th edn (Office for Official Publications of the European Communities, 1984)

Curzon, L. B., *Dictionary of Law*, 3rd edn (Pitman, 1988)

Doucet, M., *Dictionnaire juridique et économique. Legal and Economic Dictionary* (La Maison du Dictionnaire, 1979)

Fowler, H. W., *A Dictionary of Modern English Usage*, 2nd edn, revised by Sir Ernest Gowers (Clarendon Press, 1965)

Guillien, R., and J. Vincent, *Lexique de termes juridiques*, 7th edn (Dalloz, 1988)

Herbst, R., and A. G. Readett, eds, *Dictionnaire des termes commerciaux, financiers et juridiques, Tome III: Français–Anglais–Allemand. Dictionary of Commercial, Financial and Legal Terms . . .* (Translegal, 1982)

Mansion, J. E., ed., *Harrap's Standard French and English Dictionary*, Part One: *French–English*, 2nd edn (Harrap, 1939), with *Supplement* compiled by R. P. L. Ledésert with the assistance of P. H. Collin, 3rd edn, 1962

——, ed., *Harrap's New Standard French and English Dictionary* Part One: *French–English*, revised and edited by R. P. L. Ledésert and M. Ledésert, 2 vols (Harrap, 1972)

Murray, Sir James, et al., eds, *The Oxford English Dictionary*, 12 vols and *Supplement* in one vol. (Clarendon Press, 1933)

Onions, C. T., ed., with the assistance of G. W. S. Friedrichsen and R. W. Burchfield, *The Oxford Dictionary of English Etymology* (Clarendon Press, 1966)

O'Rooney, -., *Notes on the Criminal Laws and related matters in certain countries* [Unpublished multilingual glossary of legal terms, together with 'Cursory notes on some systems of law, judicatures and courts']

([United Nations] Office of Conference Services, English Section, n.d. [?1962])
*Reynolds, T., 'Comparative Legal Dictionaries', *American Journal of Comparative Law*, 34 (1986), 551–8
*Šarčević, S., 'Bilingual and multilingual legal dictionaries: new standards for the future', *Revue générale de droit*, 19 (1988), 961–78
Sykes, J. B., ed., *The Concise Oxford English Dictionary*, 7th edn (Clarendon Press, 1982)
Thody, P., and H. Evans with G. Rees, *Faux Amis & Key Words* (Athlone Press, 1985)
Walker, D. M., *The Oxford Companion to Law* (Clarendon Press, 1980)

D. Miscellaneous

*Coveney, J., and S. Kempa, *Guide to French Institutions* (Harrap, 1978)
Favoreu, L., *L'Ile Maurice* (Éditions Berger-Levrault, 1970)
Greene, G., *J'Accuse* (The Bodley Head, 1982)
Paxton, J., ed., *The Statesman's Year-Book . . . 1989–1990* (Macmillan, 1989)

Index of French legal terms